The Healing Journey to Authenticity

The Healing JOURNEY to Authenticity

Stories of Compassion, Courage & Connection

JENNIFER NAGEL

In Collaboration with Tonda Eger-Chin, Dionne Eleanor,
Sky Gerlowski, Anne Lindyberg, Anastacia Lundholm,
Lisa Manoogian, Beth Nemesh, Sylvia Schulz, and Angela Wieland

Published by Grace in Chaos Publications
in partnership with Influence Publishing Inc., June 2024
ISBN: 978-1-7753084-3-0

Copyright © 2024 Jennifer Nagel

All rights reserved. No part of this publication may be reproduced, stored in or introduced into a retrieval system, or transmitted, in any form, or by any means (electronic, mechanical, photocopying, recording or otherwise) without the prior written permission of the publisher. This book is sold subject to the condition that it shall not, by way of trade or otherwise, be lent, resold, hired out, or otherwise circulated without the publisher's prior consent in any form of binding or cover other than that in which it is published and without a similar condition including this condition being imposed on the subsequent purchaser.

Copyediting: Elizabeth Fawcett

Proofreading: Francisco Morás Castellanos

Front Cover Artwork: Vortex 3D rendering by gonin/iStockPhoto.com
Healing Hand symbol by Svetlana Parshakova/Shutterstock.com

Cover Design and Typesetting: Tara Eymundson

DISCLAIMER: This book is a personal work of non-fiction. Some of the names and identifying details have been changed to protect the privacy of individuals. Readers of this publication agree that neither Jennifer Nagel nor her publisher will be held responsible or liable for damages that may be alleged as resulting directly or indirectly from the use of this publication. Neither the publisher nor the author(s) can be held accountable for the information provided by, or actions resulting from, accessing these resources. This book is not intended in any way to replace professional healthcare or mental health advice, but to support it.

Dedication

The Healing Journey to Authenticity is dedicated to Dr. Madeleine De Little, a rare gem in the psychotherapy field, who was suddenly taken from us much too soon this past January 2024. Madeleine established Neuroscience and the Satir Model in the Sand Tray (NSST) as an innovative and creative modality for transformational change that she taught to hundreds of practicing therapists all over the world.

As one of our contributing authors in the first book of the Reciprocity collaborative book series, *Therapists are Human Too: The Healing Journey of Reciprocity*, Madeleine wrote of her personal journey to authenticity. She spoke these words when we gathered for the book launch:

My passion in life is to be authentic. I want to walk my talk and I want to walk it with my head held high. Now I can do that, and I can be with people for the rest of my time on this earth in an authentic way and be compassionate to others and support others in this work that we do. I have freedom from the shackles of inauthenticity and am able to have an unfettered future of peace, forgiveness for self, and moving forward with a peaceful sense of being able to be genuine.

This book is devoted to her memory and the difference she made and continues to make in the world.

Testimonials

We are collectively being awakened by events and tragedies on our planet. It can be hard to make sense of the chaos. This book, The Healing Journey to Authenticity, *is a wonderful guide to decoding and expanding our understanding and preparedness to heal our lives and our world—to experience the true oneness that underlies all of life, moving us closer to the beautiful experience of Sacred Reciprocity with others and the Earth.*

Kawtar El Alaoui, LL.B, PCC
Founder and CEO of Conscious Togetherness
Author of Unfolding Peace: 9 Leadership Principles to Create Cultures of Well-being, Belonging, and Peace

* * *

Life is about choice and ultimately coming to loving the one who chooses. Transforming trauma and victimhood requires a perspective of life that transcends the rational, the egoic concept of self, and the emotional framework that attaches emotions to stories. Being authentic is a journey in self-resilience, self-determination, and self-love. These stories all share aspects and takeaways that give hope and embrace the adventure.

Manon Bolliger
Retired naturopathic doctor, CEO of BowenCollege.com and international facilitator

* * *

As a leader and author of three collaborative books, I know how powerful it can be for authors to tell their stories. It is often an emotional journey, and even life changing. This book focuses on educating the reader about the significance of the reciprocal benefits of living an authentic life, and does so with a diverse range of fascinating stories. Congratulations to Jennifer who is kind, intelligent, and such a shining star in person! Congratulations to all the authors, and happy reading to you, the reader.

Rebecca Harrison
Author of the Family Tree book series
Author of *The Little Tree*, children's book
Executive Coach specializing in midlife transition

Table of Contents

Acknowledgments xi

Prelude: Expanding Reciprocity Beyond Humanity
By Jennifer Nagel xiii

Introduction
By Jennifer Nagel xvii

1 **Finding a Deeper Presence in the Jungles of Peru**
By Anastacia Lundholm 1

2 **From Dissonance to Harmony: A Healing Journey Using Metaphors of Musical Instruments**
By Beth Nemesh 21

3 **Collective Healing: Healing Ourselves to Heal the Planet**
By Sylvia Schulz 41

4 **"RISE" to Reciprocity: A Journey to Self-Discovery Through Volunteerism**
By Lisa Manoogian 59

5 **My Bullies and Me: How Bullies Supported Me in Finding My Strength**
By Anne Lindyberg 79

6 **Heartbreak: Our Catalyst for Authenticity and Legacy**
By Dionne Eleanor 97

7 Nepal to Mexico: Adventures of Personal Truth
   and Human Connections
   By Sky Gerlowski 117

8 Consciously Rewriting My Story: The Journey from Victim
    to Creator
   By Angela Wieland 137

9 Transforming Grief Through Love: A Mother's Journey
   By Tonda Eger-Chin 157

Acknowledgments

It takes a village to birth a book into the world, and there are many wonderful people to thank for their part in the process of bringing this collaborative book to life.

Thank you to Julie Ann for seeing the potential and vision of co-leading collaborative book writing retreats with me right from the start of our sharing ideas together. I appreciate your vision, your wisdom, and the unique skills you bring to getting people's stories out. I love that we can share laughter and humour together even in the midst of tight timelines and unforeseen stressors. It has been an adventure working on this project with you.

To each of the courageous authors who joined me on this collaborative writing adventure: thank you for sharing yourselves with brave vulnerability and genuine authenticity. It has been an honour getting to know you during this process, and I have much gratitude for your contribution to this book.

To the friends, family, partners, spouses, children, and community who supported and encouraged each of the authors to participate in the collaborative process of writing this book—gratitude and thanks for your blessings and support on this journey.

To Danielle Anderson, managing editor, for overseeing the editing process as a whole and your availability for input and ideas when needed. To Elizabeth Fawcett, content editor, your insight, curiosity, and wise editing suggestions allowed our stories to come to life on these pages.

To the rest of the fabulous Influence Publishing team including

Francisco "Paco" Morás Castellanos for your thorough eye in proofreading the manuscript, Tara Eymundson for the typesetting, interior design, and the cover design; I am so grateful for your part in bringing this book into world.

I want to express my gratitude for the webs of connection and experience that have inspired each person named here, for the circles of influence that have impacted the co-creation of this book project.

And finally, to you, dear reader, a huge thank you for choosing to pick up this book and join this journey with us as you read through its pages.

Prelude: Expanding Reciprocity Beyond Humanity

By Jennifer Nagel

Authenticity is about the choice to show up and be real. The choice to be honest. The choice to let our true selves be seen.

—Brené Brown

On the very first day of the writing retreat at Casa de Influencia in Puerto Vallarta, Mexico, the authors of this book were invited to open up and share with one another a personal story of how their lives had been influenced and transformed through work they had done with others and what they had learned about themselves in the process. Gathered on the rooftop overlooking the Bay of Banderas, we were gifted with hearing story after story of how family members, clients, organizations, groups, and communities impacted individual journeys of self-awareness, healing, and growth. Showing up and being real was exactly what each author brought to our circle. Vulnerably and boldly sharing our stories with one another, a common theme emerged: the journey toward more authenticity.

We reflected on the changes, shifts, and influences along our journey that contributed to our connection with the essence of who we are and how we genuinely show up in the world. Authenticity is about being true to ourselves rather than conforming to external expectations or pressures; to embrace who we truly are and to live in alignment with our core values, beliefs, and feelings. Each of these unique stories revealed the reciprocity of how showing up to serve and help others in our own way can lead to serving and helping ourselves in our personal lives.

This retreat was intended to bring the authors together in a supportive environment to begin the co-creation of the second book in the Reciprocity Series. The collaborative book series offers a collection of stories from a beautifully diverse group of authors who reflect on their personal journeys that brought about profound learnings from various individuals, organizations, ecosystems, and realms of experience. Each story underscores the giving and receiving, the receiving and the giving that loops in a multitude of directions—within, between, and among. The first book, *Therapists are Human Too: The Healing Journey of Reciprocity*, is about the reciprocity of people helping people. Social workers and therapists share stories of how their personal lives have been and continue to be transformed by what they have learned alongside the people they served.

In this second book of the series, we expand the collection to include a breadth of wellness professionals with backgrounds in therapy, business consulting, holistic health, somatic energy practices, and supporting non-profit organizations. Any profession that aims to help improve quality of life through service to, and with, others is likely to produce unique stories from those working within them who learn, heal, grow, and transform alongside the people and communities they serve—stories of reciprocity. In actuality, the people and communities we serve have also helped us in different stages of our lives and in ways we might not necessarily be conscious of.

Prelude

Having lived and worked around the globe in Canada, the United States, Mexico, Peru, Israel, Germany, England, and New Zealand, these authors impart strength, perseverance, and wisdom through a wealth of experience of diving deep to come back to Self. The chapters contained in this book offer reflection on various phases and experiences of life including healing from childhood trauma, the journey of parenthood, grief and heartbreak, exploring new purpose in retirement, reconnecting with the earth, and finding forgiveness through creative therapeutic processes. Through these stories it becomes clear that reciprocity goes beyond a person-to-person relationship and can exist between human, animal, earth, and spirit realms. Lessons can also be found in our connections with Mother Earth, in our relationship with our surrounding ecology, in societal struggles with bullying and systemic trauma (both intergenerational and national), and within spiritual realms. The weaving together of these stories form the tapestry of this book.

It became apparent as each of the authors shared their stories that they are all helping others become more fully themselves and connecting with the essence—the heart and soul—of who they are. No matter what we are doing in our chosen professions, whether it be teaching, volunteering, coaching, counselling, or consulting, the common foundation is a desire to help others connect with their authentic self and the truth of who they are at the core of their being. We are co-creating a world with more present, grounded, and engaged individuals who are able to give back in their own unique ways. By helping others with their journeys of authentic connection, we expand our own experience of Self and learn to show up with more authenticity in our lives. Reciprocity seems to be exponentially amplified in this way.

While we may have all embarked on this collaborative book-writing journey together, each one of us had to dig deep beneath the foundation of our own various roles and experiences to bring forward the stories included in this collection. Underneath these roles are roots that anchor us into deeper connection with body, mind, soul, and spirit along with an embodied sense of our greater connection to land, place, culture, and universal life energy. Too often we get caught up in the pressures of expectations, rules, and societal norms learned from childhood (many of which are outside our conscious awareness), and the patterns of survival we developed in order to meet our inherent need for connection and belonging. But by returning to these roots that connect us, we find the conditions for healing no matter what the profession.

I believe it all comes down to Love in its pure, unconditional form; Love, hope, and a desire to support people on their own journeys toward more wholeness, acceptance, and freedom within themselves.

The common hope among all of the authors in this book is to inspire others to recognize the light they bring into this world, and to amplify this light in their relationships with Self, others, their communities, this planet, and beyond. There is reciprocity in all our connections.

Introduction

By Jennifer Nagel

Reciprocity is the glue that binds relationships together; authenticity is the foundation upon which it stands.

— **Unknown**

Introduction

By Jennifer Nagel

Our existence on this planet is a culmination of and a dependence on a web of connections. They extend in a multitude of directions and dimensions including our connections with all those who came before us, our ancestry, the land we come from—indeed, all of Earth—and our current day-to-day interactions and experiences with those who cross our paths. We have infinite connections within our own experience of life from one moment to the next. Our thoughts, feelings, beliefs, and expectations are all influenced by our personal journey and the subjective meanings we've made along the way. We are also influenced by the energy we pick up from others and the resulting alchemy of what transpires when we are with others. When we really allow ourselves to think about this matrix of connection and influence, we might begin to ask what part of this experience is mine, and what belongs to someone or something else?

No matter what we do or who we are that makes us unique individuals on this planet, we are all connected through our common humanity. I have my own story, you have your own story, and yet we share the interconnection of being human. There are universal needs that everyone on this planet shares no matter our age, gender, status, or role: to love and be loved, to belong, to be safe, to have freedom and connection, to name a few. And yet, that natural desire to belong and relate to others can get in the way of living authentically and embracing who we really are in every aspect of our being.

We are born hard-wired for connection, literally depending on our caregivers for survival right from the beginning. We learn from our caregivers what is okay and not okay as far as how we express ourselves. For example, if a parent scolds their child for being "too silly," that child might learn to discount or hide that vibrant silly part of themselves. We learn which behaviours and attitudes are acceptable and unacceptable, and this tends to carry over into our adult lives as we navigate the myriad of relationships we find ourselves in—friendships, romantic partners, work colleagues, and so on. We find ourselves exploring various ways to meet our needs for connection, safety, love, and belonging. As a result, we learn to conceal or disregard parts of ourselves we believe will not be accepted or might be fully rejected and elect only to show what we believe will be celebrated or understood. We might placate others at the expense of silencing ourselves for the sake of preserving the "safety" of the relationship. Living more authentically is possible when we learn to embrace ALL of who we are. This means accepting, reclaiming, and integrating the parts of ourselves we may have neglected, connecting with each part's positive intentions and allowing them to transform and integrate, feeding our vitality.

> *Authenticity is the daily practice of letting go of who we think we're supposed to be and embracing who we are.*
>
> **—Brené Brown**

I was invited to teach a workshop in Hong Kong in 2019 on collective social trauma for front-line therapists, social workers, and crisis intervention workers. It just so happened that the region was in the middle of a political conflict between those advocating for greater democratic freedoms and autonomy versus those aligned with the policies of the Chinese government. Polarized views were impacting family relationships and friendships as loved ones were not speaking to one another if they found themselves on opposing sides.

At the beginning of the workshop, it was very evident that every participant in the room was experiencing fear, anger, and survival energy given the mixture of political views among them. The tension was thick, palpable, and unspoken in the room. I could feel my own nervous system activate in this energy and I began to wonder how I would be able to facilitate a very experiential program when there was no emotional safety in the room. These initial feelings of worry prompted me to bring my awareness to my breath, feel my feet on the floor, and send up a prayer along with the very conscious intention to show up with authenticity.

Rather than plastering a placating smile on my face and pretending that all was okay, I welcomed everyone and immediately acknowledged the differences of beliefs and opinions in the room. Everyone nodded apprehensively. Then I expressed my hope that we might connect with our common humanity first, recognizing that everyone in the room is yearning for safety, for peace, for connection and belonging even though we try to satisfy those needs in different ways, including through our political beliefs. At the foundation of life energy and core needs, we are the same. In addition, everyone was attending the workshop out of a shared desire to help others in their trauma. The group was successful in removing themselves from the context of the chaos that was happening literally out in the streets where army tankers, police, and protests were taking place because they could see each other for what they shared in that moment: the underlying humanity of desiring to help others from a place of congruence and connection.

Being my authentic self from the beginning allowed me to create a safe space within myself which made room for safety and trust among the participants of the workshop. By providing an energy of understanding, they too could hold that energy with one another and with me. From that point forward in the workshop, there was a foundation of relating with one another from a deeper place of common intentions for more peace, healing from trauma, and connection rather than focusing on differences in beliefs and perceptions. They became willing to be authentic in return and embraced their vulnerabilities in order to show up for themselves and connect with others.

> *The greatest illusion in this world is the illusion of separation.*
>
> **—Albert Einstein**

There is an element of reciprocity in all aspects of experience; we are influenced in conscious and unconscious ways by all our interactions in life, no matter how small the interaction may seem. It could be a smile from a passing stranger or the avoidance of eye contact—the "hello" or the silence. Reciprocity is in all the subtleties of our day-to-day living and being in the world. We receive information with all of our senses and we also give information in the same way. Our emotions, thoughts, beliefs, and energies of our experience are expressed in the various ways we show up for ourselves and with others.

We cannot exist in isolation from other people or our environment. The illusion of separation is just that—an illusion. We are profoundly influenced by all that surrounds us and take in information energetically and physically with all of our senses, whether we are consciously aware of it or not. For example, if someone standing in a group takes a lemon and bites into it, anyone with any prior experience of what it means to bite into a sour, acidic fruit will suddenly scrunch their face up and taste the lemon in their own mouth, even though they, themselves, did not bite the lemon. If our bodies can physiologically react in response to something we are merely witnessing rather than experiencing it for ourselves, how do we truly know what experience is our own and what belongs to other people? More importantly, how is it that we can feel so disconnected from one another and the world around us when we are capable of having such strong reciprocal responses?

We really are not as separate as we may believe.

We tend to live our human experience in the context we find ourselves in and get caught up in the status quo of the day-to-day hustle and bustle of life. We get so focused on ourselves that we become stuck in learned patterns, limiting beliefs, and old stories which result in disconnection for many people from themselves, from each other, and from the core essence of who they were created to be. Instead, we need to pause to truly be in awe of the wonder and miracle of Life and the ancestry of where we came from. What can we learn from an expanded connection with all forms of life past and present, and how do we let go of old beliefs and expectations that no longer serve us?

In the midst of the chaos that was all around Hong Kong, I looked for ways to bring in pockets of space in the workshop that could be intentionally used to find beauty beyond the participants' distress. Anthropologists have noticed across cultures that people tend to use rituals to help reduce anxiety. Rituals provide some sense of control and order for people who struggle with the unpredictability of everyday life. For this particular workshop, I introduced the idea of a ritual to bring focus and mindfulness into the room. I brought in a flower floating in a bowl of water and set it on a blanket in the middle of the room. I invited people to bring an object that symbolized peace for them and place it around the bowl. This was a beautiful experience as each person gave voice to their hopes and prayers for peace and co-created a visual centre-piece to come back to throughout the rest of the program. This focal point in the middle of our training space served as an anchor to return to a place of peaceful connection within no matter what was going on externally.

Connecting with Nature also helps reduce anxiety and regulates the nervous system. Another assignment that I gave to the participants over their lunch break was to walk through Kowloon Park, a lovely and refreshing green space in the middle of the city, and notice something of beauty. People returned with stories, metaphors, and meanings of what they found in the trees and flowers or observed in a family picnicking by a pond, a turtle swimming by, or birds singing, and so on. There was a noticeable shift in energy as people reconnected with the natural beauty of the world. While it could not take away from the seriousness of what was happening all around (every participant having to brave their way across town each morning to get to the workshop even with the constant threat of evacuation), this brief respite gave hope for better days and prevented from being engulfed by a dark cloud of despair. Seeing how the trees continued to spread their branches and provide shade, standing in peace no matter what was going on all around, was an essential part of restoring some hope and energy for the work these counsellors and social workers were doing on the frontline of the unrest.

What gets in the way of living fully as we were designed and created to live and be? What prevents us from living with more presence and authenticity? Many people seem to have lost connection with Nature, getting tangled in the wired connections of smartphones, laptops, YouTube, video games, etc. There is skepticism about what is real with all of these wires crossing and getting in the way of truly receiving. I believe there is a need to reconnect with our roots. As author D.H. Lawrence so eloquently states:

It is a question, practically of relationship. We must get back into relation, vivid and nourishing relation to the cosmos and the universe […] For the truth is, we are perishing for lack of fulfillment of our greater needs, we are cut off from the great sources of our inward nourishment and renewal, sources which flow eternally in the universe […] We must plant ourselves again in the universe.

I think of my walks along the beaches in Mexico, watching the pelicans soaring and diving. They ride the currents of air and then, spotting fish below the surface of the water, they suddenly plummet straight into a dive looking to catch their next meal. As I observe them, I am struck by the idea that they are living exactly according to how they were created to be. Wings to soar, vision to hone in on their prey as well as to spot any threats nearby, and the magnificent ability to dive quickly and precisely from the sky to the sea, resurfacing with or without their intended target. Not giving up, they once again soar until the next attempt—persistent, graceful, and fully immersed in the immediate present moment. For us to live in our fullness and how we were created to be, we must return to Nature and place ourselves again within the universe we belong to.

> *The lack of authentic connection permeates the very fabric of how we organize ourselves in the modern world.*
>
> **—Duane and Catherine O'Kane**

What allows me to show up authentically? I experience myself to be more authentic when I am in a knowing place of connection with all. It's taking the time to acknowledge and become aware of what's going on underneath my reactions and responses regardless of whether they originate from external stimuli or internal happenings within my own feelings, perceptions, expectations, and needs. And I need to be fully present in the moment while also trusting the bigger picture for Creator/God/Universe to work through me in the way that best serves. Too many people hold the perception that we are separate from earth, nature, and the universe, forgetting that we are, in fact, a part of it all. From the perspective of nondualism, all is one.

I am so very grateful for what I've learned and continue to learn from the groups I work with. There is a reciprocity of co-creating what transpires in each program. I may have a general plan for the structure of a program, but the flow of what transpires within and beyond that structure allows for the inter-play of intuition, creativity, responding, questioning, and exploring together as a group. No two programs are ever alike as every group is made up of unique individuals.

Reciprocity, the principle of mutual exchange and interdependence, shows up in various aspects of our existence giving shape and depth to our relationships with others. Expanding on this idea is the reciprocity of our relationship with the earth, sky, cosmos, and spiritual realms. It is in the giving that we also receive, and in the receiving that we are able to give. Reciprocity is the foundation for authentic connections of mutual respect and support, fostering more empathy, understanding, and trust.

This is a book about the journey to authenticity and the relationships that have been the container for reciprocal evolving, growing, and learning with one another. Each chapter takes you on a journey of self-discovery, personal growth, humility, and perseverance. My

Introduction

hope is that you, the reader, will find some gems of wisdom and inspiration in some of the stories, allowing yourself to reflect on your own unique experiences knowing you are not alone. Perhaps you will find yourself connecting with your own stories of reciprocity and ways you have changed as a result of specific relationships that have entered your life in various contexts. Perhaps your ideas of reciprocity and living with authenticity will expand in new ways as the authors share their personal stories. I encourage you to integrate what fits for you, wherever you are along your journey of healing and growth.

About Jennifer Nagel

Born in Vancouver, British Columbia, Canada, Jennifer Nagel, MA, RCC-ACS is a Registered Clinical Counsellor working with individuals, couples, and families in private practice and provides clinical supervision for other therapists. She has helped many people to show up more authentically in their personal and professional lives. An avid traveller, she teaches professional and personal growth programs using the Satir Model in Canada, China, Kenya, and Thailand.

Jennifer is a member of the British Columbia Association for Clinical Counsellors, the Virginia Satir Global Network, and is a clinical member of and Director of Trainer Development for the Satir Institute of the Pacific. She is also a senior faculty member of the Banmen Satir China Management Center. Jennifer is the author of *Magic in the Muck: Finding Grace in Chaos* and the collaborative book, *Therapists are Human Too: The Healing Journey of Reciprocity*. She is also a contributing author to *Virginia Satir's Evolving Legacy: Transformative Therapy with a Bodymind Connection*.

www.jennifernagelcounselling.com
www.linkedin.com/in/jennifernagelcounselling/
www.facebook.com/jennifernagelcounselling/

1

Finding a Deeper Presence in the Jungles of Peru

By Anastacia Lundholm

*The sun shines not on us but in us.
The rivers flow not past, but through us,
thrilling, tingling, vibrating every fiber
and cell of the substance of our bodies,
making them glide and sing.*

—John Muir, *The Sierra*

Finding a Deeper Presence in the Jungles of Peru

By Anastacia Lundholm

When the plane door opens in Iquitos, Peru, the warmth and moisture embrace me. My skin instantly hydrates and I start to sweat. This environment is considerably different from the Miami airport and the previous night's air-conditioned flight. Birds swoop and butterflies meander around me as I wait in the baggage claim area open to the air save for the roof overhead to protect from the rain. Exiting the terminal brings me into the bright sun and bustle of activity as arriving travellers are greeted and directed to their transportation. The air is redolent with burning garbage nearby, or burning brush, not sure which, maybe both. The lush green grasses squirm under the fences around the airport. The jungle may be tame here in the city, but it still has the power to assert itself in how vigorously everything grows. Stepping into the unknown, my story begins.

I was so intensely curious about how culture in my native North America affected our physicality. What would our bodies be like if we didn't sit on couches, drive cars, and watch TV but we had to make, grow, or catch everything to sustain our lives and our families? At that time, I was preparing to enter a career in the healing arts, and I wanted to know what health was, what vitality was. In order to hold a vision of where clients could grow to, I had to know the optimum end result of that growth. I was deeply skeptical that I could find examples of that in my own culture. I certainly didn't find it in myself. So, I went to the jungle to learn what it was to be human in our natural habitat. My initial goals were about this physical vitality. Later I learned there was much more to being fully alive than just our physical state or fitness. I had no idea at that time what else was in store for me to learn.

I thought I was going to learn about physical resilience. I wanted to see how the body was shaped by its environment, and how the activities of sustaining life in natural conditions contributed to strength, alignment, health, and vitality. Instead, I learned about my relationship to nature, my relationship to myself, and how adverse conditions can show us what's hidden inside us. I discovered how disconnected I was from myself and the world around me, even though I had been unaware of it. I also learned that enriching how I perceive life could help me be fully authentic. What I learned in the jungle I brought home to North America and every continent and country I have visited and worked in since. In fact, my authentic self travels with me in every part of my life now. My adventures in Peru produced one of the most profound educations I could have ever received filled with lessons to deepen and expand my experience of life; these lessons are the wisdom that I wish to share with others who endeavour on a similar journey.

Chapter 1

The Call of the Jungle

Born in northeastern United States in the region quaintly named New England, I was raised in the very conservative eras of the 1950s and '60s. My parents separated when I was quite young and my older siblings moved out around the same time. Suddenly my family went from being big, chaotic, and boisterous to very quiet as it was just me and my mom. When my mom remarried, my childhood got more complicated. There was more to escape from. I felt like I didn't really fit anywhere, even inside myself.

Somehow, I learned to protect myself from the chaos of these transitions by spending hours outside on my own. I loved treading the paths through the woods to the beach, picking wild berries, lying on my belly to stare at the microcosm in soil between blades of grass, or lying on my back to study the shapes of clouds as they moved across the sky. Nature was safe. In the outdoors, I could disconnect from all the realities of my changing life and the feelings they brought up. When I couldn't be outside, I devoured books, immersing myself in worlds that were far different from my own.

In our household there were unspoken rules, such as don't air your dirty linen in public and never hurt someone's feelings. But there were also spoken rules, like if you can't say something nice, don't say anything at all. I heard that one a lot. I learned at a young age that it could be risky to express myself. Other people's reactions could be unpredictable. Even though my gut feelings told me how untrustworthy certain adults were and gave me an awareness of the family dynamics, I felt powerless to affect anything as the adults around me didn't respond to my fears. I learned to stay small and endure. Because I was so good at losing myself to save myself, I developed the habit of disconnecting from my body and my emotions which persisted for most of my life.

When my Amazon story started, I was in my early forties. I was open to new experiences and was ready for a change of career. I was offered the opportunity to study plant spirit medicine with a trained anthropologist working with a shaman in Peru. I had no idea how this was going to fit with anything else in my life, but I felt the calling, and so I had to go. (At the time I thought it would be just one trip, but it ended up being only the first of twenty-five trips over fourteen years.) I had the desire to help others, but first, I had to help myself.

My preparation for the healing arts involved a careful summing up of the positive qualities I saw in certain practitioners I looked up to, and a list of the skillsets I wanted to attain so I could be the kind of healer I wanted to be. I made a mental list of goals without knowing how I would go about achieving them. I wanted to develop the capacity to really listen and hear someone on a deep level rather than letting my mind wander off in distraction. Even though it was often difficult to know what was happening inside myself, I wanted the ability to identify what was happening for someone else. I needed to gain more discernment about the many layers of interaction—unexpressed concerns, emotional reactions, judgments and limiting beliefs. I sought to know what was physically under the skin of another through sensory touch. I desired to ground myself in the present, and I aspired to create an environment infused with a presence that could facilitate healing. That was the hardest one: presence. I didn't even know what it meant yet, but I knew what it was when I experienced it from the practitioners whose strengths I wanted to model. Sitting with a healer who was truly present fostered a safe space into which I could relax, trust the process, and invite change.

I didn't realize how much my education would transform *me*. Stepping off that plane in Iquitos was the beginning of an unfolding of my inner defenses so I could begin to deconstruct and reconstruct them in healthier ways. In the process, I reconnected to my body and its sensations as well as my emotions and the information they contained. Feeling the warm, moist air touch my skin may have jumpstarted the sensory aspect of my journey, but it did not end there.

Embraced by the Jungle

Like any sensible North American entering the jungle, I was prepared. I had the rubber boots, the long-sleeved shirts, the sun hat, and mosquito netting. I packed insect repellant, first aid supplies, and long socks that I could tuck my pant legs into to keep the crawlies out (except the insects which I found out later would bite right through my clothes.) I had all my clean clothes packed in sealable plastic bags so if my whole duffle got caught in a downpour or landed in the river, I'd still have clean, dry underwear and socks—worth their weight in gold. But no matter how much I prepared logistically, I could never be truly prepared for the rest of the experience.

Iquitos can only be reached by air or boat. It is one of the most remote cities in the world. Going from this bustling boomtown on the banks of the Amazon to our destination in the jungle involved noisy moto-taxis, a motorboat for several hours, and then a hike through the jungle to the village on the banks of a tributary to the Amazon. As our group left behind the droning sound of the motorboat and began walking, the sounds of insects, birds and small animals surrounded us. We could hear our squishy footfalls and the rustling leaves of trees as startled monkeys moved just out of sight. The call of parrots hurtling in pairs through the air far above the trees pierced the quiet. I saw blue butterflies that magically appeared and disappeared, flitting erratically through the vegetation to their own secret destination. Their wings, blue on top and gray underneath, could only be seen when fully extended making visible the blue sheen on top of the wing. In the next moment, their wings would fold up to prepare for the next downward stroke, seemingly vanishing in mid-air. I was entranced by them.

We arrived at a nearby lodge with a palm-thatched roof and raised, wooden walkways leading to the sleeping cabins and the toilet. The jungle pushed in all around us. We arrived just before dusk and had enough time to take a short walk with our jungle guide. There were a few precious minutes before darkness came and we had to be wary of emerging mosquitos, snakes, and caimans (fast-moving animals with enormous mouths that look like an alligator only slightly smaller, with an overbite). The plants were so dense, you could get lost very quickly. We stayed close.

It seemed so different than a jungle on television; the leaves were not shiny and perfect. New growth and decay were simultaneous having never seen the deep frost of winters. But what was underfoot surprised me most. The soil I was walking on was different than back home. It was spongy and moist, as if it was nothing but composting material which, of course, it was. With each step, my rubber boot squelched deep into the decomposing duff which was a source of nutrition for anything that wanted to grow. I felt that I was standing on the lining of the uterus of the earth. This spongy layer of fertility was fed by the forest in an unending shedding of material. The rains and cyclical flooding spread the nourishment. Wherever a seed fell, it could germinate. I embodied a fetus intimately connected to its mother and was humbled by her ability to gestate everything I needed. With awe and respect for this vitality all around me, I found my relationship to Earth, our physical world. My heart and mind were beginning to open to new ways of being interconnected with my environment.

The next day I watched the cook's few chickens run around and hunt for bugs and small animals, being truly free-range birds. There was no barn yard or protective fencing to prevent them from going

Chapter 1

where they wanted. Foraging and scratching the earth, they were living their best chicken lives. One of them stopped to look up at me, locking gazes with me through its one side-eye that chickens often use. Unmoving, we held each other in a trans-species non-verbal exchange of mutual recognition of the self-hood of this bird that was stunningly deep. In a moment, the whole scene became pixelated and swirly, but for the solid clear eye of that chicken in the centre of my vision. It was like we saw to the depths of each other for a moment and the world dematerialized except for our two souls. The experience seemed sublime and ridiculous simultaneously. I didn't know what to make of that experience for a long time until I began to have that same kind of interaction with clients in the most sacred of moments. My perceptions of interconnection were beginning to open more.

During our time with the shaman, we would travel downriver in dugout canoe to visit some of the plants and trees we were connecting with. Far from a botany lesson, these experiences, among others, were lessons in being physically, energetically, and mentally present. The two-hour journey was peaceful and quiet, punctuated by the smooth strokes of the carved wooden paddles in the black water. We were five in the dugout canoe with one person paddling in the back and another in the front to clear branches or obstacles in the river. Resting my hand on the side of the boat, I could moisten my bandana and use it to cool my neck. Extra caution was always necessary, though. Before I could push off a tree when we got too close, I had to watch out for fire ants or huge thorns. The brackish water made it impossible to see the fallen trees and piranha below the surface. With barely an inch of freeboard, the slightest shift of weight could capsize us all into the river. I learned to be aware of my body and its relationship to the movement of the boat, conscious of when I needed to change position and attentive to counterbalancing the occasional adjustments of others. Together, we made up this ungainly organism. It was our collective responsibility to keep everyone dry and safe.

The beauty of the jungle was matched by the level of discomfort it caused me. I didn't know what itchy was until I had two hundred chigger bites on each foot. Sleep might be interrupted by the annoying whine of mosquitos circling my head inside my sleeping net, and the itchiness that signaled they had already found what they were looking for. Being horribly overdressed by day, unwilling to expose my pale flesh to all the hungry mouths that wanted to eat it, resulted in a sweaty mess of muddy clothes that stuck to my damp skin. A quick shower in river water in late afternoon was heaven. I had to have a flashlight to go to the bathroom at night because there was likely to be a small animal either in the toilet or eating the bar of soap provided; there were always teeth marks on the soap in the morning.

The discomfort from heat, itching, and uncertainty brought my emotions to a head. There was no option not to feel them. When the physical body and emotional limits are challenged through heightened stress, the mind struggles to cope while uncertainty and irritation can take over. I felt misunderstood or wronged at times. It was easy to project hurt feelings and frustration onto others. The emotional pressure would build and build toward some kind of dissipation or release. As I look back now, I see a lot of those emotional reactions were similar to how I might have experienced them as a child not being able to express myself in words.

On successive trips, I saw this process of emotional struggle in others. Most times we would welcome a small group of students who were all healers in some capacity wanting to deepen their personal work through the teachings of the shaman and the plants. Students often had varying levels of ease or distress at the beginning of each trip. I took time to come together as a group to cooperate and understand how to be in this new environment and context. Eventually, many of them would reach a point of overstimulation and have some kind of meltdown resulting in yelling, stomping, anger, or tears. These strong reactions would usually be volatile and brief and, immediately afterward, we could all see a shift in the person. Their eyes would look bright, clearer, and open. There was a softening that took place. Their faces relaxed and their body language would exhibit more ease. Frustration would be replaced by a sense of acceptance. The jungle herself was the biggest teacher; she would force us to our limits of tolerance for discomfort, uncertainty, and sensory stimulation. The people of the jungle, the plants, and the process of entering their energetic world changed us.

For those of us who came from North America, there was a big cultural shift that was required to not only be respectful to our hosts, but also to fully engage with the lessons we were there to learn. Mostly this involved decreasing the amount of talking and thinking we did and improving our ability to feel and notice things around us. That's it in a nutshell; I learned to listen more, talk less, and notice things. Whether it was the wordless hierarchy of who showered first, the necessity of using as little water as possible so everybody was able to get clean, or feeling the energetic summons to meals, I was being asked to leave my own dreamy world and truly immerse myself in my surroundings. It was important to notice every little thing, including when to come to the table. The information exchange became increasingly nonverbal. Energetic messages were every bit as important as verbal ones. We had to learn to attune to the pulse and rhythm of the group, the village and nature herself. The more I returned to the jungle, the more I learned to trust my instincts and the deepening of my sensory perception with people and the environment.

It was this energetic messaging that I needed to develop a relationship with each of the plants I was studying—a relationship that grew slowly over many years. Building a bond with the plant was required before we were allowed to ingest anything. It would take years to sense the qualities of a plant or tree as each plant had its own purpose and personality. Sometimes the plants would teach us in dreams, sometimes in visions while dozing in a hammock, or sometimes through messages in words or images while in direct contact with the plant. My acquaintance with different plants would expand from year to year. Each time I returned to the jungle, my relationships deepened, both with the plants and with the shaman and his extended family in the village. It was this ongoing process that allowed me to grow in so many ways and achieve the goals I had set for myself before I first travelled to Peru.

Bringing My Wild Self Back to North America

My adventures in the Amazon were demanding. The rigours of travelling, the heat, and the itching were just the beginning of discomfort. There were also the intricacies of cross-cultural interactions where my actions would have unintended meanings for those of another culture. Later on successive trips, I would be responsible as a cultural interpreter for those experiencing Peru for the first time, and I was learning as I went. Being in such a different environment than I was used to startled me out of habitual ways of thinking and doing. Moving beyond my habits helped me be more aware of myself, my feelings, reactions, intuition, and insights. In the process, I became more authentic with myself. There was no other choice. The jungle, the shaman, and the villagers offered me new, intense experiences in which I had to pay attention to myself, others, and the environment. I learned that things I might do without thinking in my own culture, like pick up a piece of litter, had repercussions in other's perceptions of me and meanings made. I learned that it was the equivalent to visiting someone's house and cleaning something as if the environment was not clean enough for my standards. I learned to slow down and be mindful about how every action might be perceived.

Each time I returned home, I found my senses heightened from my experiences in the jungle. I would feel more and have a greater awareness of the interconnectedness of things around me. I would have to relearn how to manage these new levels of sensory processing and the information coming to me. My body gave me so many messages and I was able to hear them. In my daily life and work, I learned how to make use of my new skills and to practice them in my local environment. The intense pressures of the jungle sped up my learning process, but the lessons became more meaningful when I was able to integrate them into my life at home.

As my energies and emotions transformed bringing me closer to my true self, I felt apprehensive about returning to my North American life. The friction between the highly-sensitive me and the former people-pleaser me who put myself last created a dissonance I couldn't ignore. It was a strong wake-up call to resolve the parts of my life that were incongruent or intolerable when I was "fully awake." At times when I couldn't bear to be inside, I would go hiking to reconnect to the balm which was nature's embrace, take silent walks in the forest or park, or just walk around my neighbourhood. I'd allow myself to hear all the layers of sound from wind to birds and small animals to people. Attuning to sights, sounds, smells, and signs of life helped me be more present to the environment. I would take the time to notice the plants, even the weeds, and acknowledge the different flowers, grasses, or trees as individuals.

Feeling my body sensations as I walked helped me be aware of my feet on the earth, what the soil or pavement felt like, as well as noticing my breathing, the beating of my heart, and the feel of my muscles as they got warm and supple. Recognizing these body changes helped me be in the moment wherever I was. Being completely present, I could identify sensations that would draw my attention to something. I remember a small grouping of young oak trees that attracted me. When I stopped to tune into them, a feeling of teenage exuberance and joy came over me. I also recall a particular book on the bottom shelf in a bookstore that just grabbed my attention. When I picked it up, it was a unique memoir of a Buddhist monk that had insights for me on my journey. And sometimes, standing in a crowd, I would just have a general feeling of goodwill that I wished toward everyone, and someone would turn around and look directly into my eyes with an expression of recognition.

I remember being in sync with the sun, waking and sleeping naturally according to the sunrise and sunset, making it hard to stay up late with electric lights imitating our natural solar illumination. I recall getting messages from plants in public places asking for care and nurturing and trying to find socially acceptable ways of tending to them and answering their call. In many ways I was now an integral part of the environment in which I found myself instead of floating through the world separate and distracted. It felt so other worldly to begin to see and feel more than is commonly felt, seen, and talked about.

The gifts I have received through the years since gaining this knowledge have been many. Paying attention to myself and what I am experiencing has helped me be more aware of my internal world—my reactions to things and my feelings about them tell me to pay attention and make the choices for me. My internal sense of what is uncomfortable or what feels right is the most important barometer I possess. This sense is incredibly important to me in my work when I consider options and use my intuition to guide me in any particular moment.

Orienting to the context of my environment helped me be more present in various surroundings including my work, travel in different countries, and navigating the nuances among people and cultures. My sense of others and being able to attune to what they might be experiencing has helped me become a better listener and friend. When I work, I begin by centering myself and preparing myself to enter someone else's energetic space. This may only take a moment, but it is one of the things that allows me to be fully present with another in a way that is supportive, hopeful, confident, and accepting. This process inevitably leaves me feeling even more grounded and resourceful when I finish work than when I started. I ultimately receive the gift of my own presence when I am present as teacher or coach for another. It means I can give clients my full attention and, together, we can find a way forward that suits them. Being intentional with how I am being has, over the years, reinforced and deepened all the learnings I received in the jungle.

Lessons From the Jungle

You don't have to go to the Amazon to gain what I gained. You can sharpen your senses in any environment by paying attention and relating to what is around you. I sometimes instruct my students to find a plant in their home or office that is there to support them or that they like to have around. I instruct them to spend a few minutes looking at it, making a connection with it by appreciating it, and then sensing what it needs: perhaps to be turned, repositioned, watered, or tended to. Taking time to send messages of appreciation and gratitude offers a way to acknowledge the interconnection that you have with this other living thing. We are all here to care for each other and connect with one another. Perhaps there is a plant on your balcony, windowsill, or outside your office that you walk by hundreds of times. Think about saying hello next time. One day you might get a greeting back.

To be present requires focus. You can lose focus by being distracted either by your own busy mind, or with the outside stimulus you use to fill the space in your awareness. It is so easy to slip into its temptation too. I often find myself turning on the radio or a podcast while doing housework, for instance. It takes me away from the tedium of day-to-day tasks, but I lose the thinking time and the clarity that comes from processing all the things going on in life. This processing and clearing of mental clutter makes way for creativity and original thought. In the jungle, I had zero distractions. There was no escape from the challenging moments I had to face, but I'm far richer for the experience.

To increase the use of your senses outdoors, skip the podcasts or conversations while you walk, garden, or hike. Be in silence for a few minutes, or longer. See if you can be in silence as you go towards your outdoor destination, or at least until you arrive. Can you stay in silence for the whole time you are in nature? What happens? Feel into the environment—it is full of life! You are inside it, not just passing through it. Become even more aware of the varying air temperatures, breezes, sounds, and energies. Start to ask yourself some questions:

- Is there a place that calls you?
- Is there a plant or physical feature of the land that gets your attention?
- What happens when you stay connected with it for a few minutes, or longer?

Staying in connection with all of your surroundings is excellent training for your senses. Your openness and perception will expand. Attune to the sounds in your environment. Really listen.

- Can you hear the wind?
- Can you hear the sound of birds? Which ones, and how far away?
- Do you hear really quiet sounds that you don't usually pay attention to? Notice how the sounds change while you are walking.
- If it rains, how many different surfaces does the rain strike on its downward path? What sounds occur when it hits them? How many kinds of drips and splashes do you hear? When we just hear "rain," we miss the music in the storm.

Once you have developed this awareness, you can start applying it to other situations and interactions. When something unexpected happens and you notice and acknowledge your discomfort, it can help you be honest with yourself about what you are experiencing. So often we disregard or ignore our natural responses. Feel the feelings, listen to your thoughts, notice and evaluate them. Are they justified? Is there more behind them? This kind of emotional and intellectual honesty with yourself creates a pattern of being authentic with oneself. That is the foundation upon which you can build authenticity with others.

Your most challenging environments are your laboratories. In my native New England, we had two settings: stuff it and seethe, or blurt out and regret it. I've learned that there are many more choices and possibilities when it comes to dealing with our emotions. We can assess them and recognize them. We can process them by speaking them aloud to ourselves or channeling them through art, journaling, music, or movement. As you learn to discern your authentic emotions and your reactive emotions, you will be better able to cope with stress and chaos. Observing yourself when you are reactive can shine a new light of awareness on the instinctive response. When you are aware of your internal experience you can be more compassionate to yourself and more in charge of the process. Eventually during stressful times, you may be able to acknowledge your emotions and let them flow through you without being overcome. By attuning to your inner experience and your environment, you can gain an authentic way of walking in the world. Your self-awareness, awareness of others and awareness of your environment can increase the presence you bring with you everywhere you go.

When I was a child, lying on my belly fascinated by the microcosm of life in the soil, staring at clouds or wandering the forests and beaches in New England, little did I know that nature was helping me, soothing me, and calling me home to myself. Maybe she is calling you too.

Chapter 1

About Anastacia Lundholm

Anastacia Lundholm has been teaching body-centred personal growth internationally since 1998 through workshops, classes, one-on-one coaching, and retreats. In 2005, she added the Satir Model to her theoretical framework and has since begun offering training through several Satir Institutes internationally. An instructor in Satir Transformational Systemic Therapy for the Satir Institute of the Pacific, she received their 2023 Leadership Award.

Anastacia trains therapists, psychiatrists and social workers in China and Thailand to integrate body awareness, experiential exploration, and use of the body into the therapeutic process. Her goal is to enhance everyone's ability to interact with their clients in the journey toward self-responsibility, congruence, and transformation. She is a contributing author of "Bodymind Wisdom in Satir's Model" in *Virginia Satir's Evolving Legacy: Transformative Therapy with a Bodymind Connection*. Her work has taken her to seventeen countries on the continents of North America, Europe, South America, Australia, and Asia. Anastacia lives with her husband and their parrot in Bellingham, Washington.

anastacia@bodymindfulwellness.com
www.linkedin.com/in/anastacia-lundholm
www.BodymindfulWellness.com

2

From Dissonance to Harmony: A Healing Journey Using Metaphors of Musical Instruments

By Beth Nemesh

It is a joy to be hidden,
and disaster not to be found.

— **D.W. Winnicott,** *Playing and Reality*

From Dissonance to Harmony: A Healing Journey Using Metaphors of Musical Instruments

By Beth Nemesh

What if you experience your mom as a Grand Piano, and your dad as a Trumpet?

Children's initial experiences in life are through sound, touch, and movement. These experiences impact the ways they make meaning and understand the world and themselves. Auditory and visual memories can be powerful.

My childhood was complicated and can be best understood in connection to the story of a client named Willow. Working with her using musical sculpting helped me redefine who I was as a person and clarify my unique professional modality.

As a young therapist practicing in both music and family therapy,

I struggled to define my professional identity. I wanted to construct an integrated model to combine my dual expertise. Thinking creatively and out of the box, I was particularly drawn to experiment with Virginia Satir's family-sculpting by adding non-verbal information through the use of musical instruments. In selecting a musical instrument to symbolically represent a specific person, we create a distance where it is safe to express oneself about that person. More so, our choice includes unconscious characteristics and knowledge we are not aware of. The instrument can replace a direct verbal description when it is insufficient to convey the multifaceted experience and impact of that individual, including their sensory and energetic aspects, as well as visual and auditory memories. Soon I would see the impressive power of family-musical sculpting on healing past injuries, family relationships and early childhood trauma, both for my client and myself.

Willow

Given the importance of Willow's story to my own, I am recounting it as she has shared it with me. At the time she came to see me, she was in her early twenties.

I am Willow. When I look back through my eyes as a small girl, my memory is of Dad mad and shouting. Yelling loudly in short sentences. Starting in low tones and climbing in glissandos. Loud and impatient. Hollering short orders and creating chaos in the room. Throwing things and banging. The walls were shaking and echoing over and over.

My hands were on my ears and my eyes were shut really tight. Now the sounds were muffled, but my body reverberated with the vibrations absorbed through my skin. I was shaking, cold, frightened, and alone. Mom was in the room, and yet she had nothing to say.

She did not help me or defend me. She was silent. I was drifting in my imagination to a forest, flowing water, riding on a cloud with the music of the wind.

Only now, twenty years later, I am ready to face my past. Maybe it is time for me to open my eyes, allow myself to hear, find whatever I am looking for, and let go of the fears stored in my anorexic body.

My siblings all have college degrees and have successfully moved on to create a life of their own. I feel like a failure. I feel alone and unloved. My dad's words keep haunting me: "You are stupid and worthless! Why can't you do this right?" I also remember my mom's silence—a void I couldn't and still can't understand. I don't know what she was thinking or feeling. She was physically present, but at the same time very absent.

I am a musician. I create songs and compose melodies that touch my inner pain, though I never expose them to the outer world. I cannot express or show my vulnerabilities to others. I am voiceless, a mute musician tangled in the past. Only now do I realize how much of my silent mom may have become a part of me.

Here I am, trying to untangle my memories and stories, trying to understand what happened to me in my childhood. What is keeping me stuck in a frightened child's body with no voice?

Willow's Family-Musical Sculpture

I had been working with Willow for a while to create a timeline of her life experiences. We gathered her fragmented memories, making sense of their impact. We had formed a trusting relationship and a musical connection. Sensing Willow's struggle to find words to describe her family and their dynamics, I decided on a new nonverbal and unconventional approach to further her progress.

I asked her to create a family-musical sculpture.

Family sculpting is how family-therapist Virginia Satir played out the dynamics and communication styles of the families she treated. She used body postures, gestures, position, and height to create a family sculpture that could experientially demonstrate their relationships, alliances, power struggles, distance, and roles. In family-musical sculpting, a client chooses a musical instrument to represent a family member, using the instrument to project their own unique meaning, feelings, thoughts, and memories of that family member. An instrument, whether actual or imaginary, can be chosen for any of its characteristics—sound, rhythm, material, size, color, resonance, or the way it is played. This method provides clients with new information and awareness of the person they may have difficulty communicating with as well as incorporating detailed unconscious knowledge to reveal more than words can say.

This was my initial use of family-musical sculpting. I had been thinking about the possibilities of this technique for a while, and I thought Willow would greatly benefit from it. I believed it might help clarify her childhood experience and allow subconscious information to surface.

First, I asked Willow to choose a musical instrument to represent each of her parents. She began by choosing a Trumpet for her dad. She explained that he is very loud. She continued to describe the sounds of the trumpet as a series of very loud, short staccatos rising in glissandos from the lower notes to very high and sharp shrieks. There is no melody. He sticks the trumpet right in other people's faces, including her mom's face. Her dad's trumpet is long and protruding, very much like a male representation. His use of it reminded her of an assault. She explained that he plays the trumpet with one hand while the other is being used against others.

For her mom she visualized a Grand Piano. She described a huge instrument that is taking up a lot of space in the room. Her strings are limp and have not been tuned in a long time. Her pedals are broken. Her winged top is shut, and she is covered with dust. She is silent. Willow barely remembered the tunes it once played. A grand reminder of lost memories.

I asked Willow to create a musical dialogue between her parents. What would it sound like? Willow held an imaginary trumpet in her hand but couldn't blow into it. She teared up and cried. She curled into herself, like a butterfly in a cocoon, hugging her petite body and rocking herself back and forth for comfort.

After a while she opened her eyes and looked at me with a sad expression. She said, "I can't do it. I can't be this kind of person," while pointing to the trumpet.

She took a deep breath and then turned to her mom's instrument. She got up and walked to the piano. Gently with soft strokes, her hands drifted over the keys making no sound. She spoke to her in a quiet very low, soft voice: "Oh Mommy, this is so sad. I remember when we all went together on nature hikes. You loved nature, and you loved to sing. You gave us names that are connected to nature. You knew so much about flowers and trees. You sang to us when we had a hard time walking, so we could keep up with Dad's pace. What happened to you?" At the last sentence she looked up at me, as if I would have an answer.

Willow covered the piano with a soft blanket and laid on it, hugging the piano.

"Poor Mommy, what you had to go through in your life with Dad until you decided to leave him and save yourself. You were so scared of him, and stayed with him long after he robbed you of your voice. I never understood your silence. I wanted you to stand up to him and say something. Anything.

Poor Mommy."

An Empowering Song of Anger

Willow arrived at the next session with more energy than usual. She said, "I had to write a song for my dad about how scary he was, and how he made me feel small and incompetent. Everything I never told him… nor anyone else."

First, she carefully went over the lyrics with me, accentuating the words which were significant to her. She then sang the song as she played an acoustic steel-string guitar. Her music was louder than ever before. The melody she chose, a simple structure of easy chords, became a mere vehicle to convey her powerful words. Her lyrics blamed him for his abusive behaviour and for not seeing her: "No one deserves to be treated this way." She sang about growing up alone with fear and shame. Her voice was clear and angry while the metal strings highlighted the loud, clear, sharp notes.

She shared with me that she had never before admitted or exposed her anger and fear towards her father. She said that it felt good and empowering. I felt the pride she experienced and shared her new smile of satisfaction. Willow continued: "After I wrote my dad's song, I wanted to write a song for my mom. This was so much harder and heartbreaking. There is so much that I see now that I did not realize before. I see how my mom accepted my dad's abuse so that he would leave us children alone. Especially me. Now I can see her silence in a different way."

Additionally, she pointed out that she noticed how she and her mom were in many ways very similar, and that it was extremely hard for her to admit this to herself and to me. She continued to share: "For a long time I hated her. The way she did not react, say something, or defend me. There was always a tension and distance that I sensed between us. There were no hugs or comforting words. I felt she was cold and distant. As a child, I believed that I was the problem, and that my dad was angry because of me. My mom was not there for me. From a very young age, I went out of the house and walked in the forest for hours until it became dark, dreading coming home."

A Song of Sorrow and Forgiveness

At the next session, Willow walked straight to the piano and once again put the soft blanket over it, this time adding several stuffed dolls to rest on its top. She sat and played Mom's song—a sad, slow tune like a lullaby song in sweet minor chords. Very softly and gently, she sang. The words were about understanding her mom and forgiving her. Willow's body was relaxed and as soft as the melody. Her voice was flowing, warm and clear. In this song, the words were few and simple, but the melody carried the longing and wish of the little girl within her for her mom.

Reflecting on the music and the lyrics, she pointed to the similarities between herself and her mom: their mutual love for nature and music; both losing their voices out of the fear of repercussions. While creating the music, she realized both of them did not have a mom figure present in their life. She could now see her mom as a strong, good, and resilient mother; in contrast, she still perceived herself as weak and invisible. There was an underlying yearning to discover those positive qualities within herself.

Willow noted her new understanding of her mother's situation as a "parental child" in her own family of origin. As the oldest of many siblings, Willow's mother took on the role of caring for the younger children learning to place others before herself. She was a placating partner trying to avoid conflict at any cost, as well as a mother who repeated the same appeasing patterns of coping she had internalized as a child.

Again, Willow sat at the piano repeating the song with tenderness and sadness, a harmony between her and the music of the Grand Piano. She continued to sit at the piano long after the sounds faded. Relaxed, quiet, with her eyes tearful and shut, she focused on the quiet energy of the music as it gently echoed between us. There was a sense of peace within her and between her and her mom.

Willow named this song *It's Not Your Fault*. It is a song about forgiving and having compassion for both herself and her mom.

A New Professional Identity

This trial of my family-musical sculpting intervention had been an incredible success. Family-musical sculpting actually worked. My sessions with Willow showed that this is a deep, experiential, and impactful technique that helps uncover and connect to the unconscious memories we hold. It was everything I hoped for.

Creating this technique was a defining moment for me, clarifying my professional identity as a family-music therapist. I felt light within me as I realized these sessions with Willow had highlighted and resolved my need for a clear professional identity. It felt right.

While working with Willow I was consciously aware that her personal adverse childhood experiences triggered similar experiences in my life as a child. This might have led to an unconscious identification with Willow which reflected in our close therapeutic alliance. I needed to be consciously aware and mindful that her therapeutic work was not about healing my own wounds.

I was encouraged by her experience to address my own historical wounds using family-musical sculpting. I hoped that through the musical sculpting experience I could gain new insight and awareness of my childhood, make peace with my past, and let go of my anger.

Chapter 2

Choosing Compassion over Anger

Once I decided to construct family-musical sculptures of my own family, I realized that I have always unconsciously known my family members' musical metaphors, as if they were visually and musically embedded this way. I had always been known as the angry child. "Mad" and "Bad" were my nicknames. If I was to give up this anger, which felt like a significant piece of my personal identity, what would be left of me? It was in a conversation with a relative that my perspective changed. Reflecting on how she remembered me as a child, she told me, "You had character and guts… And now, maybe it is time for you to know your worth without needing their approval or needing to prove your value over and over. Accept that you are fine just the way you are." After that, letting go of my anger was no longer associated with becoming weak, or losing my power or energy, but was now about being more confident and in harmony with myself. Finally, it was time for me to resolve my historical anger.

I was willing to use family-musical sculpting to try and figure out who I was without the profound anger that had defined me since early childhood. I had already begun Buddhist psychotherapy studies in conjunction with pursuing this journey, and I hoped this technique would help me gain a compassionate perspective of my past and the people who were part of my life experiences. It made sense to me to exchange my anger with compassion and understanding, both towards myself and then towards others. This was a journey I could take now that I finally understood there was something to gain, not lose.

Creating my family-musical sculpture was a gamechanger. It is described below using notes I made from the recording and my recollections in the moment. It includes my experience of the musical expressions, the metaphors and sounds, my thoughts and sensations, feelings, body messages, and images. Mainly, the new awareness and meaning I gained through the process.

A Duet of a Solo Flute and a Sad Guitar
My dad was represented as a Pan Flute—the kind that is played with a lot of air, sounding hazy and foggy. The melody was sweet, light, and fast yet with a disorganized rhythm and melody. He played random notes in a lovely exploratory tune. Much like the Pied Piper, his melody enchanted people around him. I envision him walking forward, leading others who followed him as a leader and a legend. They admired him never questioning his motives and intentions. He had plenty of charisma, creativity, imagination, fun, and passion. He was also smart, sophisticated, and had great social skills demonstrated by the audiences who adored him. Yet he seemed to have no grounding and no responsibility to others. He never even looked at them.

At home, there was another side to him. The sculpture brought up memories that I had forgotten, and probably wished to forget. I remember him being abusive, neglectful, shady, self-centred, and lacking integrity. Many of us were hurt by his actions and behaviours, all masked by a facade of justifying explanations. He was not a person for accountability or admitting a mistake. I had not forgotten ways he deceived me just so he could always be right, or how I believed him and cooperated with him. I conceded that the salt in the pancakes was better than sugar (when he mixed them up), or that the lumps were just the way pancakes should be (when he didn't bother to stir the batter). While listening to the recording, I noticed my anger towards him had a new added sadness. I felt sad for my childhood naïveté as I understood and accepted that as a child, I had every reason to adore him, to believe he was telling the truth, to not doubt him but doubt myself. Now I feel sad and sorry for him, as well as angry.

Chapter 2

My sculpture developed as I went on to create a musical dialogue between us. I was a tuned Classical Guitar with nylon strings and a mellow tone. It might seem on the outside that we were compatible, both being soft, melodic instruments. In the sculpture, he was leading with his usual cheery, jumbled pan flute melody. As I was trying in vain to find a way to join his disorganized song, he pried the guitar from my hands. Then he played my guitar. Now the strings changed from plastic to metal strings, louder, untuned and with an annoying buzz. He was showing me how to "do it right." He never noticed that I didn't have a role or any place in this so-called musical duet, or that it sounded awful. I remember similar feelings in my past, where I never said a word to him about how I felt, and how his music sounded. Again, he was content with his own perceived perfect sound.

As I internalized this information from my musical sculpture, I realized how accurately it represented our relationship and communication. It was always all about him being in the centre. I could still feel my anger towards him in my body, my emotions, and my thoughts. I still hurt. Something more was needed to let go of the anger.

I tried to use plenty of self-compassion towards my child self along with accepting his crooked personality so I could let it go. It was an acceptance of what was. The knowledge that I was smart for figuring out his lies even though I assisted in hiding the truth about him from others. I knew that being on his side made me feel more special, more loved. I could recognize that trying hard to defend him made me a strong and determined child.

It was only when I wrote my anger into a song, putting it on paper and then voicing it, that I could let go of the anger, shame, and regrets I had about him, about myself as a child, and about our relationship. Writing, singing, and playing those emotions were the experiential aspect that enabled a deep transformation of my anger directed both at him and at myself. Consequently, I was able to become more compassionate to myself as a child, and compassionate and accepting towards who he was, with all of his faults.

As he got older, having developed a debilitating illness and having been rejected and robbed from his wealth and fame, I took him into my home and cared for him until he went to a nursing home. I did so without anger or resentment. I cannot say I loved him, but I figured out love needs to be an experience based on mutual respect which I did not have with him or for him. At the end of his life, he often mentioned the pain he caused to so many people around him, including me, my mom, and my siblings. He died sad and lonely with many regrets.

This is how I remember him.

Healing a Heart of Swiss Cheese

In my family-musical sculpture, my mom was a Horn—the kind depicted on the head of the Devil. The sound was high pitched, piercing, stable, each sound accented with a marcato. It gave the sensation of being pierced. The target for these sounds was my heart. As a child I couldn't explain to others that my heart was like Swiss cheese with many holes. I know they are there and that they hurt, but I knew that no one would believe me. I remember telling a friend who was afraid of his dad's belt that it is so much better to have a red mark that shows than holes in your heart that no one could see. I couldn't understand how I didn't bleed to death.

Our musical dialogue ended before it started. The idea of any connection or musical exchange between us paralyzed me. I couldn't get close enough for us to play anything together, nor could I find my voice. Memories of our relationship surfaced during the sculpture, including one where I tried to test her love and concern for me.

Chapter 2

Leaving the window of my room slightly open to give the impression that I jumped out through it, as I often did, I hid inside the linen closet staying silent, waiting to see if and when she would notice I was gone. I was heartbroken to find out that it took several hours. My sister came looking for me and announced that I wasn't in the room, and that was it. I was not found. It seemed to me that my disappearing had no significance or impact on my mother. I stayed there for as long as I could only to eventually come out feeling transparent, broken, angry, and devastated.

Many years later these memories were still vivid. I feared her and hated her for controlling (or trying to control) me and for comparing me to my fairytale sister who was a perfect, placating child living up to my mother's expectations. I felt alone. Whenever I was noticed, it was usually for something bad or extreme.

This new information from the sculpture sent me on a journey to discover more about my mother. I needed to understand her background, where she came from. I needed to see her as a human being so I could come to terms with her and my past. I asked her questions about me as a baby, a child, and a teen. It seems that I had always been a handful. My mom, like many other parents in the '50s, raised us according to the popular, and often strict, guidelines of raising children. My sister was a perfect baby who read and abided by the rules. I, on the other hand, was hungry at the wrong time, cried endlessly, and refused to be consoled without being picked up (an action which was considered needless pampering, causing children to develop bad habits). My mom had back issues, meaning she couldn't and wouldn't pick me up. So I cried. My mom never said this in a straightforward way, but I understood I was a challenge, a difficult child who did not obey the written book for raising children.

I believe there was a lot of frustration for her as a mom with two children and a bad back. I also became more aware of her own childhood upbringing which included having a dysfunctional mom and a hard-working, absent dad. I realize now that she did the best she could under those circumstances. She was always there to provide us with everything she believed that we needed as children. She made us eat healthy food, she kept us clean and neat, and she taught us and modeled healthy values. What I lacked in my childhood was warmth: to feel appreciated, supported, and loved. I now understand that she was focused on our survival and meeting our basic practical needs. I believe that she could not provide me with the emotional support I needed as she had not received emotional support in her own family-of-origin.

I realized how history repeats itself in our parallel stories of three generations of the women whom I knew in my family, starting with my grandma, my mom, and me. Most shockingly, I realized that I am repeating this in my own life with my children making me the next generation of emotionally distant but practical mothers. This was extremely unsettling for me, and it made me ever so sad. I was sad for my mom, for me as a child, and for our relationship. Sadness overcame my anger towards her. Expressing this sadness, I played the sad tune from *Forbidden Games* on my guitar in dedication to the strong and sad women of the family.

This is how I remember her.

Willow: "Accepting and Loving Me"

"I am the Guitar and the singing voice. I tune my guitar. I know the music and know the lyrics, as they come from and are within my heart. When I play my guitar, I am alone with my pain and sadness…"

My heart skipped a beat as I recognized me in her.

I felt my body crying with her, for her, and for me. I felt like hugging her, like hugging me. I was aware that what she and I needed was closure and consolation…

I asked her to write a song about who she desires to be. In minutes, she wrote a simple song with simple minor chords. She sang the song using soft, slow strums on the guitar.

Just being me,
Accepting and loving me,
Quiet and loving
Accepting and loving me.

I joined her, creating mutual harmonies pausing on "accepting and loving me," experimenting with vocal harmonies, dissonances, and improvisations until we are both in peace and smiling. There is a new quiet and peacefulness in Willow.

It was time for us to say goodbye. Willow's hard work led to her pursuing a musical education and taking a step into creating her own future. Her smile and the gleam in her eye showed me she was ready to go on without the baggage of her past controlling her life.

She shared that the sessions that helped her most in her transformation were the family-musical sculpture ones, especially the Grand Piano experience. She learned to see her mom in a new, compassionate light. Willow has allowed her mom back into her life and continues to rebuild a healthy relationship between them. Her dad moved on and is barely in touch. She feels relieved that she is no longer anxious about him.

Harmony

The resemblances between Willow's childhood experiences and my own exist on many levels even though our stories are unique. I am happy Willow is taking this next step into life. We had a short, meaningful, and profound journey together. Now it is done.

Willow's musical metaphor, her words and melody, and our mutual harmonies touched me deeply. There is magic in a musical connection. A duet of two voices creating harmonies is like the two wings of an eagle. A gliding sensation of connection, majestic spirituality, and trust. I felt my soul being freed in the process. Thank you, Willow, for your part in my life and in my journey for growth.

Finally, I could transform childhood memories stored within me as anger and bitterness to compassion and acceptance of myself and others. I now hold feelings of anger and bitterness in a place where they cannot be harmful. A place in a healed heart that does not hurt any more.

It felt like I was putting a blanket of a soft lullaby on my aching, injured heart and soul. Something in me had changed. I was no longer frightened of what was to become of me without my anger. I was not afraid I would be weak. I was at peace within myself. I was softer though stronger.

Now I had my own journey to take.

Without my blinding anger, I could see my mom as a human being. I became aware of her own baggage and history. She had done her best to raise me with the little family support she had, and with what experience and knowledge she had. There was no more anger and blame.

I respect and admire my mom for what she accomplished in her life: the hardships she had to overcome raising us kids after my dad left, her values as a strong and independent woman in control of her life, and the way she puts family first. I can see the true care and concern she has for me, then and today.

I acknowledge the ways she has changed with her grandchildren. She is softer, more loving, and easily hugs them. Since making my family-musical sculpture, I am less triggered by her natural criticism of us. It might still be there, but I am more balanced and compassionate and do not resort to my childhood defences of blame and anger.

Coda

Today, my mom is a Marimba—a blend of a percussion instrument and a soft melody. It brings out the tones of the earth with her warm wooden sounds, mellow, rich, and deep. She resonates with soft and gentle harmonies. Her melody is slow-paced, steady, and clear. She takes her time with every strike of the soft-padded mallets. Sound blends to sound, resonating and creating blends and overtones. Her music has become a soft blanket.

That is how I will remember her.

I hope that one day I will have those deep and warm sounds as well.

About Beth Nemesh

Beth Nemesh, PhD, MT-BC, LMFT is a licensed Creative Arts Therapist majoring in Music Therapy, a licensed Family-Marital Therapist, a Clinical-Supervisor, and a Body-Mind Psychotherapist who integrates Buddhist philosophies with Western theories. Graduating from Satir Transformational Systemic Therapy (STST) training under Dr. John Banmen & Dr. Nitza Broide-Miller, she was drawn to Virginia Satir's basic beliefs and the experiential, positive, humanistic foundations of the model.

Beth is committed to integrating Expressive Arts (music, movement, visual art, photography, bibliotherapy, psychodrama) with family therapy and the Satir Model, teaching Arts Therapists the importance of a systemic approach, and highlighting the impact of our family of origin on our health and well-being. She helps families, couples, individuals, and groups to become more confident, competent, and congruent. Beyond her private practice, she teaches, conducts workshops, publishes articles, presents in conferences, and is a co-founder of Satir Institute of Galilee in Israel (satirglobal.org/institutes-affiliates/).

www.bethnemesh.com
www.linkedin.com/in/beth-nemesh-phd-mt-bc-lmft-91b78a91
bethnemesh@gmail.com

3

Collective Healing: Healing Ourselves to Heal the Planet

By Sylvia Schultz

*The ecosystem tries to heal itself through us, as us.
We can choose to collaborate with that
self-healing mechanism,
but often we don't want to feel the discomfort of
our unintegrated past.*

—Thomas Hübl

Collective Healing:
Healing Ourselves to Heal the Planet

By Sylvia Schultz

Changing my career as a secretary to work within the medical, spiritual, and energetical field began with a question. At the age of thirty-six, I was sitting with a group of women whom I had been meeting with once a week to help organize the local school's bazaar. One of the women told us that she was diagnosed with cancer in a health checkup. We all were shocked given how healthy and strong she seemed. We didn't see her for a couple of weeks while she completed the treatments her doctors recommended. The next time we saw her, she was a shadow of her former self. She looked thin, weak, pale, and seriously ill. As she went through course after course of treatment, it was hard to ignore that her health seemed to worsen every time she was in treatment. Sadly, about a year later she passed away.

The Healing Journey to Authenticity

I couldn't help but wonder what would have happened if she had never learned of the cancer at this checkup. Unable to get this question out of my head, I started investigating cancer. One thing led to another and shortly after I started training as a holistic cancer consultant with Lothar Hirneise, a worldwide expert in the field of cancer therapy.

This was the beginning of a long road toward learning techniques and modalities in the area of energy healing and holistic therapy. I studied and completed my exam in 2010 to become a Naturopath and ran my own practice until December 2021 when I decided to move to Mexico. I do believe that the only true healing is self-healing. This is what I teach in my classes and sessions. My medical knowledge helps me to understand the physical ailments my clients are experiencing, but healing is so much more than getting rid of body issues. I love the way that energy healing has an impact on the body and vice versa.

Today I work as a facilitator for people who sense a calling to a higher purpose but don't know where to start. They may be bored, depressed, unhappy, or in a place that no longer works for them. I help them connect to their internal knowledge through the wisdom of their bodies, become aware of thoughts, feelings and emotions that do not belong to them, and find their own path to explore who they really are. I also work with people who have significant health concerns to assist them on their journeys. To be diagnosed with a serious disease like cancer is a loud wake-up call. My job is to create the non-judgmental space in which they can meet themselves.

I believe that acknowledging the energies that surround us is crucial to understand our bodies, our lives, and the world. It is my passion to explore how everything is connected and interacts with one another. What if you could change everything that is not working for you?

Chapter 3

Wake-up Call: Feeling the Energies around Me

When I was thirty-five-years-old, standing in the busy shopping area of my hometown Ravensburg, Germany, I suddenly realized that I could not see colours anymore. All of the people walking past me on this sunny, early, spring morning looked ugly and grey. My beautiful medieval hometown lost its vibrancy and charm. While I didn't call it depression at the time, I knew these sensations in my body were a reflection of my state of mind.

I thought to myself, *this has to change*, only seconds before thinking, *I don't want to live anymore*. It popped up for only a nanosecond in my awareness but was immediately dismissed; it was not an option for me as I was a mother of two amazing little sons. They were my everything and I would never have chosen to leave them behind. The mantra "this has to change" repeated in my mind as I searched for what to do next and who I could talk to. Suddenly I thought of my former college and dear friend, Waltraud. She was in the middle of shamanic training, and somehow I knew that she was the person I needed to speak with.

There were no cell phones at the time, so I had to wait until I eventually got home to call her. She agreed to give it a try and we settled on a time she could work on me with an energy healing session. During the session, I laid down on the couch. Shortly after beginning, I had a strange feeling in my chest like somebody was stirring my insides with a spoon. It was a strange and wonderful feeling at the same time. It was the first time I witnessed consciously my heart open without any external trigger. I started to feel love and gratitude toward everything around me. The feeling was so strong and radically different from what I had felt a couple of minutes earlier that tears began running down my checks and my face started to hurt from how much I was smiling.

Waltraud told me after the session that my heart chakra was totally blocked and standing still. Unblocking it changed everything for me. When my husband came home that night, he was very surprised about my change. From that moment on, I could clearly see that how I feel is not dependant on circumstances beyond my control. It was up to me to care for my energy body as well as I do my physical body. It was my first profound experience in healing over distance. I began acknowledging my body's wisdom even though it would still be a long journey to fully trusting its signs and signals. In this moment, I knew I had always felt energies strongly even though I hadn't realized it. As these energies felt normal for me, I had thought it was the same for everybody.

Following this healing experience, I began reflecting on several incidents in my life where I either listened to or ignored my body and what resulted from it. For example, at the age of nine I had to have two surgeries after a skiing accident. I pretended to take all the pills the nurses gave me but threw them in the toilet as soon as I could walk on my crutches. I didn't have an opinion on medication at the time and it was not something that was discussed in my family. I had no information at all about alternative medical care. But for some reason, my body clearly said "no." I likely wouldn't have been able to swallow them even if I had tried. This is something I clearly wouldn't recommend to anyone. But, at the time, it seemed to be the thing to do.

After the first surgery, my hay fever started shortly before Christmas and continued through a very cold and snowy winter. I had the snuffles for weeks and then it intensified when everything started blooming in the spring. I was diagnosed as having allergies. My mother found it strange as the symptoms started in winter, but nobody really investigated. It took decades for me to realize that this diagnosis prevented me from acknowledging what it really was: an overdose of toxins, most likely from the anesthesia. Right after the surgery, I vomited for the entire day. It wasn't until I began treatments to detox my body, learned through my naturopathic training, that my allergy symptoms disappeared, and I realized how they were connected to the toxins. This also explains why my body insistently said "no" to the pills—body wisdom.

Asking a lot of questions can lead to the root cause of body symptoms or blockages. Exploring the energy underneath the spoken words and the information our bodies give us through the limitations and sensations they currently have is the foundation of my practice. Listening to the energies around me and to my body led me on a personal path of healing that I knew could also help others access their own innate knowledge.

Bodily Perceptions: What is your body telling you?

As a child we know what our bodies are telling us. Reminding ourselves of this knowledge and trusting the signs and signals is a choice and, from my point of view, one of the greatest adventures in our present time. Many people I work with have forgotten about this ability, at least partially, having grown up in a society that tells you what to think, feel, emote, and do. From a very young age we are trained to ignore the body's needs and requirements rather than to fulfill them. At the same time, most of us experienced our awareness being constantly questioned, or told it was wrong.

Think about your experience as a child and the information you were told by parents and teachers. If you had an invisible friend you talked to, you may have heard, "Oh, this kid has a strong imagination, how sweet!" Maybe you were afraid in certain rooms of the house or around certain people. What were you being made aware of? It could have been an entity or the energetic imprinting of an argument or violence. You knew when you entered the room that your parents had an argument, but instead they told you, "It is nothing, sweetie, all good!" Incidents such as these are how you started to trust others more than yourself. You love your parents, you trust them, so how could they lie to you? You might even have done that to your own children in trying to protect them. Instead of judging yourself you could acknowledge that you have a different choice now.

I have always been highly aware of the feelings and emotions of people and animals. One of my first memories as a kid around three-years-old involved a trip to the zoo. A baby elephant had been separated from its mother and left outside of the elephant house, most likely for some sort of treatment. I remember clearly feeling the despair and fear of the little creature in my body. I cried my eyes out the whole car ride home.

While this may seem like a small, irrelevant story, these stories have a way of adding up. It's not just a feeling; it's a perception of another creature's emotions that I was able to receive through an awareness of my body. It wasn't until 2016, after almost fifteen years of being on my spiritual and holistic healing journey, that I learned that 98 percent of our thoughts, feelings, and emotions do not belong to us. What? In the first Access Consciousness® class I took called Access Bars®, I found the missing link. This information started changing everything for me as I considered the repercussions. It took a while to understand the magnitude of it. All the stress, the sadness, the depression, the confusion, and the anger that I still sensed were there after almost twenty years of energy work were not mine? Oh my god, if that was true… Looking back, so many things suddenly made sense to me.

For example, twice in my past I encountered the deceased body of an individual after committing suicide. Both times I experienced shock, fear, and panic, but the first time this happened, I judged myself tremendously for it. I was sixteen at the time and it was the mother of my boyfriend. She died of an overdose from alcohol and

Chapter 3

drugs while we were out, and it was me who found her the next day. I was paralyzed by fear the following days whenever I was in the apartment. I felt pathetic having reacted so strongly. Today I know why I did. My body was giving me information about her violent death.

The second deceased individual I found was a beautiful young lady laying peacefully on a bench near a creek. While walking my dog, I came across her. I felt the same fear, confusion, and shock as before. But this time, I had the tools to handle the situation. I knew to ask myself "who do these emotions belong to?" The answer came back to me clearly that it was the entity, forcefully torn from the body. Having been taught how to communicate with entities that I perceive, I was able to address the entity and help it move on. I know now that I perceived the shock and the confusion of the entity still there. I have spoken about this topic to others who didn't really believe in the spirit world, but while discussing it, they would recall an experience they've had in the past that was similar. Even if you never considered it possible, by increasing your body awareness you might experience something in your world, for example after a loved one passed, that could change your perspective.

By asking the question "Who does this belong to?", I have been able to identify which emotions are not mine to send them back to whom they belong to. This has brought a lot of ease and peace to my life. Everything that is true for you should feel light, bright, and uplifting in your body, even when something is not positive for you. Whatever is not true for you will make you feel heavy. I use this method all the time to determine if something is true for me or not. Once the heaviness disappeared, I would realize it was not my feeling or emotion, but a sensation that my body received which wasn't mine. Playing with this tool for a while changed a lot for me. It was a relief to learn that many of the things I could not change in my life did not belong to me in the first place.

I invite you to give it a try. When you wake up next time feeling depressed and stressed, ask yourself "Who does this belong to?" or "Is it mine?" Often these questions alone make you feel lighter and happier because you no longer accept this mood as yours. You can send all the remaining heaviness back to the rightful owner. And don't worry, you won't make someone depressed or angry by doing this. You cannot change what does not belong to you. So return it to the person who can change it.

You can use these questions to get more information from your body. If you have a sudden headache, knee pain or something similar, ask your body, "What are you trying to tell me?" Play with it and start treating every sensation in your body as a message to tell you about something. Many of these messages will not be relevant to you, but some are. It may not be useful to know that the stranger on the bus has knee problems, but a sudden flutter in your body while your children are playing in the garden by themselves could be very important.

These perceptions in our bodies could be more than what others around us are feeling. At present, many people are experiencing nausea, pain, heart palpitations, headaches, and other symptoms that seem to have no physical cause. What if these symptoms are a sign of the trauma and healing of the earth itself? Is now the time to acknowledge that our individual healing capacities includes healing the spaces around us? What else would be possible if this became common knowledge? How much healing could occur for us and for the earth?

We are amid a huge transformation. I am convinced that it is the time to start incorporating our body's knowledge into our lives rather than handing it over to experts who repair our bodies like broken watches after ignoring it for so long. You are the expert for your life and your body. Visit doctors and therapists to help you check in with your body on what is going on, but do not exclude your own perspective of what you feel, sense, and know.

Collective Trauma: Is It Time to Radically Heal?
What if you have post-traumatic stress disorder just by living in this collective reality?

One reason why people are so focused on experts outside of themselves, not daring to speak their truth, are the collective traumas we have developed through culture histories and societal norms. There were times where it was not safe to stand out in the crowd. Instead, we learn to fail with the group rather than follow our knowing and risk standing alone. Many of the coping mechanisms we developed just to survive are not even a result of traumas and experiences from this lifetime such as abuse or car accidents. They are programmed through collective traumas that originate in our ancestors and are passed down over generations. The fear to be seen, to speak our own truth, or the lack of feeling secure are often symptoms of inherited trauma that is deeply connected to and stored in our bodies. Every culture has some form of collective trauma; in my case, being German, it was the trauma of the Holocaust.

Born in the sixties in Germany, when many communities were just beginning to remove Nazi-affiliated teachers and politicians, my own path of healing led deep into the history of the atrocities of Nazi Germany. Not very interested in what we were being taught in school, I began reading book after book of personal stories about people and their experiences during the Holocaust. Like many other girls, I was deeply touched by *The Diary of Anne Frank*, and Judith Kerr's novel *When Hitler Stole Pink Rabbit*, but I didn't stop there. For more than twenty years, I read every book on the topic I could get my hands on. I wanted to understand what it takes to become a perpetrator, a follower, and a victim. What made ordinary people follow this cruel and insane man who organized the industrial killing of millions of people? Why did they look away when their former neighbours where robbed, violated, and deported? How were they okay with that, or how did they accept it? Why would they assist in this and denounce people who were part of their lives until then? What kind of propaganda and manipulation tactics were required to allow one man and his henchmen to not only start a world war, but also build this system of racism and antisemitism that was the foundation of the genocide that followed?

To process my country's immense trauma that, in the beginning, I bought as my own personal trauma, I tried various healing modalities to address it. For many years I fought for justice against war, violence, and environmental pollution. But the more I healed, the more I realized that the only way to really change things was by helping create a different world. This is what my work is about: creating a reality on planet earth that supports people to express their uniqueness and live in community with the planet. A world in which people do not have to kill themselves or one another because they think they have no other choice. A conscious world in which people do not embolden or follow leaders who support war.

Collective trauma can also be felt within our society as the shared fear of judgment. If someone is in a mainstream profession doing tasks that are widely considered as beneficial and acceptable, they will feel strong and self-confident. As soon as they start to do a profession or run a business that speaks directly to their own heart, that changes how they perceive themselves. They may feel called to bring what they know to the world but getting it out and taking the risk of being judged is scary.

Andrea, a client whose name I changed to keep her anonymous, works as a controller and one of the CEOs in a medium-sized company. She had no fear of speaking up and being uncomfortable in her working environment. When she started taking a lot of classes with me and other facilitators, her professional life and her work environment changed a lot. The other CEOs had no idea what she did differently, but they saw that her attendance resulted in more effective meetings, that individuals in those meetings felt acknowledged and heard, and the outcome was beneficial for the employees as well as for the company. The business target numbers increased even in economically difficult times, and she found she had a good intuition about what projects were worth supporting financially. Although Andrea felt that she was near the end of her career in this company when she started the classes, she ended up skyrocketing in her field and her sense of fun and fulfillment came back to the job.

Given the success she had experienced with the tools she learned, Andrea had the desire to add "stress coach" to her resume in order to bring this knowledge to other companies. But showing up to speak to people about this topic was totally different than walking into a meeting in her former company. While she felt the stress of her own anxiety and fear of judgment in this new role, she had to lean into the discomfort in order to follow her true calling. Oftentimes people believe they must be ready and fully prepared to start something new, but nothing would ever start because we always learn through doing the thing that we start. One of my coaches once said: "If you are not embarrassed after coming out with something new, you have waited too long to start it."

What makes it so difficult to follow these paths? For centuries, so called "witches" were persecuted in various countries around the world. They were killed for being different and having abilities no one else seemed to have. While this may be an obvious example, there was no past society that celebrated or tolerated differences. Going against or choosing something radically different than most of their contemporaries was dangerous. To this day, it is still a brave act to choose your own path according to your knowing. Doing it, though, brings you a level of joy and freedom that nothing else can give you.

Healing this collective wound through acknowledgement, clearing techniques, and body work is the key to change. Moving forward and processing what is coming up on the way is essential. In my country, it is obvious that as a collective body, we have by no means fully processed this trauma. There is a lot of work to do. But implementing clearing techniques together with conducting body work can create miracles.

Clearing the Trauma: Presence is the Key to Awareness

Presence is the ability to process every experience in the same moment that we go through it. And it is the key to be able to perceive what really is. This takes us out of thinking about our past, whatever successes or failures may have occurred, as well as out of the worries of the future. What else would be possible if we stepped out of the survival mode caused by past traumas and instead felt secure and nurtured on our beautiful planet? In order to have access to your knowing, presence is the key. If your attention is in the past, the future or in somebody else's reality, you assume what is going on rather than perceive it. This assumption is based on conclusions, judgments, and expectations instead of awareness. Acknowledging your awareness is a muscle that you must train to be able to use it to your advantage.

My first boyfriend died in a car accident after we split up. I was eighteen years old. I ran into him in a club by accident the night before he died, and we had a terrible fight. He didn't want to accept that it was finally over. A couple of hours later, on a straight stretch of highway, he crashed his car into the only tree in a huge meadow.

Chapter 3

He and his passenger died while another was seriously injured. After he died, I could clearly sense his presence in the days leading up to his funeral. I had no doubt he was there. The awareness was crystal clear. At the time, I felt I didn't have any tools to deal with this awareness and I added some drama instead to my perception. I was convinced that he was there to get me having made it very clear that he refused to be without me. I had no clue with whom to talk about this and I was trapped between my grief and my angst.

What would being present in this situation have looked like? I took the guilt into my body because I didn't want to deal with it. If I had told anyone, they would have told me that it was not my fault. This was not what I felt. I couldn't handle it, so I hid it deep in my body. In an ideal world, had I been able to be present in that moment, I could have said to myself: "Okay, I feel guilty. No matter if I am or not, I have to handle this now to get free. I don't have the tools or the experience to handle this, therefore, I need help. Who can help me with this?"

Fourteen years later in my first spiritual class, I was finally able to let his entity go. For all those years, I was not aware that I held onto him through my feelings of guilt over his death. After the funeral, I shut out my awareness of him as I could not handle it. I had blindfolded myself against perceiving what I knew to be true and now I held the information required to finally let him go.

Through my clients, I can see that not wanting or being able to deal with the consequences is one of the main reasons people will be unaware of something that is blocking them. If you unconsciously assume you do not have what it takes to handle it or if you are concerned of the consequences, you lock your awareness out which prevents you from being in a present state. What would it take to say: "Okay, I am aware that this relationship, this job, or this place is no longer working for me. But at the same time, I do not want to

55

or cannot change it now, because I do not want to accept the consequences that I know of right now. What else is possible?" And then let go. Don't look for the answer in your mind. You won't find it there. It will come to you in the most random ways. Be ready to receive it, even if it looks different than you thought it would. Acknowledging what is not working for you without the need to react sets you free.

Access Consciousness is about "living in and as a question." I always had a hundred questions to one answer, but with the Access tools I learned to cultivate asking real questions: "Who does this belong to? What else is possible? How does it get any better than this?" are some of examples. Who would you be without the beliefs and definitions of yourself, and the conclusions you have? Undoing belief systems and automatic answers opens the door to infinite possibilities.

You Are a Healer

According to my belief we are tiny parts of the universe, expressions of the longing of the whole to experience itself. We are part of the ecosystem of earth and part of the cosmos of the universe. With our beautiful bodies, we can experience what pure energy can't. We can feel wind and rain on our bodies, swim in the ocean, smell flowers, taste food and drinks, as well as cuddle and have sex. We can experience pure joy along with pain and suffering.

What if there is no good or bad in what you experience? No better or worse? Just an experience? There will never be another you with your unique point of view. You add your individual experience to the field of collective information—sometimes called matrix, quantum field, or morphogenetic field, depending on who is talking about it. For example, there are reports of apes living on an island that have started to wash their fruits in the river and use a tool to open them. If a hundred apes do that, the apes living on other islands will start

Chapter 3

to do this as well. This is because they added their experience to the field. At one point every ape has access to their experience through the field. This is also how it works for us.

I am sure you experience the contribution of the earth and nature when you are amid a healing process. The earth heals, transforms, nurtures, and relaxes you. In nature you can let go of the pressure, the discomfort, and pain as the earth takes it and transforms it with no judgment.

Did you ever consider that it could also work the other way around? You can be a huge contribution to the earth and its current healing and transformation process. Each time you let go of a collective or personal trauma, the earth sighs in relief. Your personal energy has an impact on the earth's journey. Each time you choose healing instead of fight or flight, you contribute to a future planet worth living in. What energy are you choosing today to add to the whole? What if the pollution, the environmental disasters, and climate change are not the disease but the symptom of something underneath, like a tumor is a symptom asking for attention? What if it is anger, rage, fury, hatred, and the need to be right that is killing the planet and collective trauma is the root cause? The world is asking for change.

We are all one. There is no separation. All things are connected. When we heal, we heal each other and we help heal the planet too. It all starts with listening to our bodies.

About Sylvia Schulz

Sylvia Schulz is a Naturopath and facilitator working in the field of energy healing and coaching. She closed her own naturopath practice after ten years to move to Mexico in 2021 and now offers sessions and mentorship programs to women who follow their calling, acknowledge their purpose, and live up to what they are here for.

Sylvia was born in Ravensburg, a small town in the south of Germany, in 1967. Having been a shy and introverted child, she transformed into a rebellious teenager and later to an inquisitive adult who knows that there is so much more possible than this reality tells us.

As an empath and highly aware of other people's energy field, Sylvia learned through various modalities to cultivate and train these abilities on her own healing journey and now teaches these tools to her clients.

Her vision is to help create a more conscious reality on planet earth where people are empowered to be who they truly are and to let go of collective and personal trauma in order to heal not only us, but also our beautiful planet.

www.sylvia-schulz.com

4

"RISE" to Reciprocity: A Journey of Self-Discovery Through Volunteerism

By Lisa Manoogian

*The world is full of good people.
If you can't find one, be one.*

— Unknown

"RISE" to Reciprocity
A Journey of Self-Discovery
Through Volunteerism

By Lisa Manoogian

Life's twists and turns often lead us down unexpected paths, don't they? My husband and I thought we had it all figured out when we bid farewell to Chicago in 2018, ready to embrace retirement life in the sunny paradise of Puerto Vallarta. But as fate would have it, our journey took an unexpected detour when we stumbled upon RISE (Refugio Infantil Santa Esperanza) Children's Shelter, a place that would redefine our notions of purpose and community.

When we first crossed paths with RISE, we saw it as a chance to fill our days with meaningful activities. Little did we know it would become the heartbeat of our new life in Mexico. Amid the vibrant chaos of the shelter, we encountered stories of resilience and hope

The Healing Journey to Authenticity

that touched our hearts in significant ways. As newcomers to the world of volunteerism, we quickly realized that our ways of operating an organization were vastly different from the methods employed in Mexico. In the face of this cultural divide, we learned the invaluable lesson of patience. It was a lesson that would shape our interactions with the children, the staff, and the broader community.

But here's the beautiful thing about reciprocity: it's a two-way street. As we navigated the challenges of cultural differences, we found ourselves coaching as much as we were learning. Our experiences in our corporate and entrepreneurial jobs in the United States had equipped us with a unique set of skills and perspectives that we eagerly shared with the team at RISE. We quickly learned that there is a different way to work in the Mexican culture requiring us to embrace uncertainty and celebrate diversity in all its forms. For example, communication has been a real challenge for us. It's not just about our Spanish skills; Mexican culture tends to avoid directness to spare feelings. Clear communication is critical for any organization's success, but particularly for RISE, so we've had to get creative. We've learned to ask questions in different ways to really understand what's going on. What used to frustrate us has taught us to be patient and adaptable. Together, we embarked on a journey of mutual growth and understanding, transforming RISE into a beacon of love and acceptance within the community. In the sections ahead, I invite you to join me as we explore the transformative power of reciprocity and the boundless potential of human connection. For in the end, it's the relationships we forge and the lessons we learn along the way that truly define our journey.

Chapter 4

From Chicago to Puerto Vallarta: A Journey to RISE

Our journey to Puerto Vallarta and involvement with RISE Children's Shelter began with a simple suggestion from a friend who wintered in this picturesque city. Over the course of three years, we visited him for long weekends, soaking in the warmth of both the sun and the community. It was during one of these visits that he planted the seed—suggesting that we consider retiring in Puerto Vallarta. Intrigued by the idea, we decided to test the waters and spent three months here in February 2018. Eager to give back to the community that had welcomed us so warmly, we turned to social media, posting a request for volunteer opportunities with children. Feeling strongly that children are the future of our community and the world, we want to give them the best possible opportunities in life. They deserve all the love and support they can get.

That's when we stumbled upon RISE Children's Shelter, under the care of two dedicated nuns—one of whom was the founding nun and director of the shelter. They had their hands full with thirty-five children. The first day we stepped into the shelter, we received a text just five minutes prior warning us that the kids had lice. Uh-oh. We were greeted by eight-year-olds who showed us their middle fingers. In that moment, we couldn't help but wonder what we had gotten ourselves into. Despite the chaotic start, we chuckled and pressed forward.

An English program for toddlers was just being launched, and we jumped at the chance to get involved. Starting with two days a week for two hours, we found ourselves falling in love with these little ones. We spent hours scouring the internet for toddler-friendly craft ideas and embarked on scavenger hunts around town in search of supplies. Being new to both working with kids and to Puerto Vallarta, we found ourselves asking, where does one even find contact paper, pipe cleaners, popsicle sticks, and the like? Even larger stores like Walmart didn't have all the supplies we needed. It wasn't until our second year in the toddler program that we stumbled upon a treasure trove of crafting materials in places called papelerías.

As our three-month stint came to an end, we knew in our hearts that we had to return. Heading back to the United States for six months, we eagerly awaited our chance to come back and volunteer. Upon our return in October 2018, we resumed our roles teaching English to toddlers. But word got out about my husband's restaurant experience, and soon we found ourselves helping with fundraisers. It turns out, having restaurant experience is incredibly relevant to fundraising events. Whether it's planning, organizing, or preparing for cocktail and dinner gatherings, the skills and expertise gained from running restaurants are directly applicable. As we became more involved, we began helping in many different areas. We're helpers by nature, and it felt like a natural fit.

During this time, we decided to make Puerto Vallarta our permanent home, purchasing a condo and fully immersing ourselves in the community. In the summer of 2019, changes to the board of directors at RISE prompted a call asking if we could lead some of the committees—kitchen, volunteers, and fundraising. Without hesitation, we accepted, becoming more entrenched with the kids and the team at RISE.

Then came the unexpected curveball of Covid 19 in 2020. With all the volunteers gone and us living in Puerto Vallarta, we found ourselves stepping into roles we never imagined; from maintenance to IT services, we were there to support the shelter in any way we could. With masks, smocks, and shields, we followed strict Covid protocols, continuing to help the children who needed us more than ever.

Tragedy struck in August 2020 when our beloved director, Madre Mari, passed away after battling cancer. Due to the rules of the nunnery, Madre Leti, the co-director, was unable to stay on the premises without another nun, requiring her to depart soon after. In the scramble to find a new director, we stepped up to support the interim director, offering guidance and assistance wherever needed. When he departed a year and a half later, we found ourselves continuing in our supportive roles, eventually welcoming the current director in November 2022.

Today my husband, Bill (Memo), and I are deeply involved in the operations of RISE. I serve as the treasurer, while we both sit on the board, oversee and recruit volunteers, lead fundraising efforts, and are involved in the day-to-day activities. It's been a journey filled with unexpected ups and downs, but through it all, we've found purpose, community, and the true meaning of reciprocity.

RISE Children's Shelter: Nurturing Hope and Resilience

RISE was founded in 2001 by a nun and a priest with the hope to bring shelter to the vulnerable children of Puerto Vallarta. Having the capacity to house up to fifty children, RISE serves as a refuge for those who have faced neglect or abuse in their young lives. There are currently twenty children living at RISE from the ages of two months to eleven-years-old—and this changes daily. These children come to RISE through the family arm of the government, Desarrollo Integral de la Familia (DIF), after being removed from their homes due to various forms of mistreatment. The spectre of physical, sexual, or substance abuse looms large in many of their pasts, leaving indelible scars on their innocent hearts. Some arrive at RISE straight from the hospital at birth, while others find their way here at different points in their childhood.

At RISE, these children find more than just shelter—they find a home imbued with love, compassion, and unwavering support. The dedicated team of fifteen full- and part-time employees, including nannies, a driver, a cook, cleaning staff, a director, a teacher, and a psychologist, ensure that their every need is met. The operation runs around the clock with three shifts of caregivers, providing a nurturing environment 24/7. Even with this help, the shelter is always on the lookout for experienced child trauma psychologists who are fluent in Spanish. While RISE has been fortunate to collaborate with a few local experts who offer invaluable training to the staff, finding additional professionals in this field remains a crucial aspect of our mission.

In addition to the committed staff, RISE relies heavily on the contributions of volunteers to enrich the lives of the children under its care. Volunteers engage in a variety of activities aimed at fostering growth, learning, and joy. From providing English lessons and playtime for the nursery children to organizing donation drives for food and household items, each volunteer plays a vital role in creating a supportive community within the shelter.

The array of volunteer-led initiatives encompasses everything from academic support to creative expression. After-school programs offer homework assistance and literacy lessons, while arts and activity sessions provide opportunities for self-expression through art, dance, music, and cultural exploration. Martial arts classes, storytelling sessions, and catechism lessons round out the diverse range of activities available to the children, ensuring that their days are filled with both enrichment and joy.

Volunteers not only engage in activities with the children but also assist in organizing donations, maintaining the twenty-three-year-old building, and facilitating food donation deliveries and preparation. Despite my husband's ironic lack of handiness, he was assigned the role of maintenance lead. However, he has effectively assembled a skilled team of volunteers capable of handling electrical, plumbing, and construction tasks, ensuring the smooth operation of

Chapter 4

the shelter.

Every Saturday morning, the kitchen crew enjoys their workout routine by hauling boxes of soon-to-be-expired fruits, vegetables, and other items up the fifty steps to the kitchen. They then meticulously sort through the donations, ensuring that only the edible items are retained.

Despite the essential services it provides, RISE operates solely on private donations and fundraising efforts. While the government oversees certain aspects of the children's lives, such as interactions with family members and adoption proceedings, financial support for the shelter remains absent. As a result, RISE relies on the generosity of donors and fundraising activities to continue its mission of providing a safe haven for the children of Puerto Vallarta.

At RISE, we understand the importance of providing a structured environment for all children under our care. However, we recognize that children who have experienced trauma require even more consistent and predictable routines to feel safe and secure. This structured environment serves as a lifeline for these children, offering a sense of stability and predictability in a world that may otherwise feel chaotic and unpredictable. From the moment they wake up to the time they go to bed, our children follow a carefully planned routine that guides their day. This structured approach not only helps them feel grounded and supported but also alleviates the anxiety and uncertainty that often accompany trauma. Whether it's preparing for school, engaging in educational activities, or enjoying playtime, each aspect of their day is thoughtfully structured to meet their unique needs. The sense of safety and security that is created through this environment allows these children to focus on their growth and development without the constant worry of what might happen next and, ultimately, reclaim their sense of hope and endurance.

Additionally, it is important to recognize that many of the children who come through our doors have experienced significant trauma which can deeply impact their ability to learn and thrive. Despite their innate potential, the scars of their past often manifest in academic struggles, making it difficult for them to succeed in traditional school settings. Compounded by the necessity to place children in grades aligned with their age rather than their academic ability, many find themselves in classrooms where they struggle to keep pace.

Imagine a ten-year-old child placed in the fifth grade and expected to navigate lessons and assignments without having acquired basic literacy skills. It's a scenario that underscores the urgent need for tailored intervention and support. That's why, at RISE, we've developed a volunteer-based literacy program designed to meet the unique needs of these children.

We are very fortunate to have two very dedicated volunteers with child education experience who created our literacy program. Because of them, children can embark on their journey to literacy at their own pace in a safe and nurturing environment. Rather than being overwhelmed by material beyond their grasp, a ten-year-old may start with first-grade level books, gradually building confidence and proficiency as they progress through the curriculum. The children are given an opportunity to develop foundational reading and writing skills that lays the groundwork for future academic success.

By meeting children where they are and providing personalized support, we aim to break the cycle of academic underachievement and empower each child to reach their full potential. Through the transformative power of education and compassionate care, we strive to create a brighter future for the children of RISE.

At RISE, every effort made by our committed staff and volunteers is fueled by a singular purpose: to provide the children under our care with a fair chance in life. Whether it's through nurturing their academic growth, supporting their emotional well-being, or simply providing a safe and loving environment, our collective aim is to empower each child to overcome adversity and reach their full potential. We believe that every child deserves a fair chance at a bright and promising future, and it's this belief that drives us to do everything in our power to ensure that they have the support and resources they need to succeed.

Fundraising: Paving the Path to Sustainability

When my husband and I first dipped our toes into the world of fundraising for RISE, we were fueled by a desire to make a difference, yet admittedly, we were somewhat naive about the extent of the shelter's financial needs. Our journey began with events like the cocktail and appetizer soirée at the stunning Demetro Art Gallery. Although we initially focused on creating memorable experiences for attendees rather than diving into the financial intricacies, it wasn't long before our fundraising responsibilities began to evolve.

Initially there required more time and coordination as opportunities presented themselves in unexpected ways. We were invited to be the charity of choice by the manager of The Palm Cabaret and Theater for their opening night, where donations for entrance were given to RISE. Further bolstering our efforts was the generosity of an individual like Big Jack, who came into RISE one day offering to orchestrate an international dinner on the beach, preparing food from various countries. Two hundred people were in attendance! These events, though modest in scale, laid the groundwork for what was to come. As the pandemic gripped the world and traditional fundraising avenues became restricted, innovation became our ally. Inspired by a volunteer couple's suggestion, we ventured into the realm of online cooking classes, featuring a renowned local chef Sol

Rose, to engage supporters virtually. While these endeavours proved successful in their own right, it became evident that RISE required a more strategic and sustainable approach to fundraising.

Enter "So, You Think You Can RISE" (SYTYCR)—a brainchild of ours born out of a desire to harness the immense talent of Puerto Vallarta while generating crucial funds for the shelter. Modelled after the popular talent show *America's Got Talent*, SYTYCR aimed to showcase emerging talent in the community while simultaneously raising awareness and funds for RISE. As newcomers to organizing an event of this magnitude, we collaborated with local theatres to host the preliminary rounds and utilized social media, flyers, and posters to recruit talent and spread the word about the shows. The local media played a crucial role in promoting the event, and their continued support has been invaluable. Key contributors to the success of the event were the dedicated teams at Colectivo Hueco, led by Tirso and Lucero, Tracy Parks at Incanto, and Mark Rome of The Palm Cabaret, who provided invaluable guidance and support throughout the process.

Despite facing numerous hurdles, from theatre closures due to hurricanes to ongoing Covid-related restrictions, SYTYCR persevered. What began as a modest venture quickly blossomed into a celebrated annual event, drawing crowds of nearly 800 attendees to its grand finale in both 2023 and 2024.

The impact of SYTYCR extends far beyond its entertainment value; it has become a lifeline for RISE providing a substantial portion of the shelter's annual budget. With a current budget of $3,500,000 pesos ($200,000 USD), necessitated by the growing needs of Puerto Vallarta and rising costs, SYTYCR has become instrumental in ensuring the shelter's sustainability. At the most recent grand finale, we proudly shared RISE's compelling story with the audience, raising an impressive 60 percent of our financial requirements—a testament to the unwavering support of our community.

As we look to the future, SYTYCR stands as a beacon of hope symbolizing the transformative power of collective action and the boundless potential of philanthropy. Through events like these, we continue to pave the path to a brighter tomorrow for the children of RISE, ensuring that they have the resources and support they need to thrive and succeed.

Personal Transformations: A Journey of Growth at RISE

My journey at RISE Children's Shelter has been nothing short of transformative, reshaping my life in ways we never could have imagined. What began as a simple desire to give back to the community has blossomed into a deeply enriching experience that has touched every aspect of my being.

First and foremost, my time at RISE has instilled in me a newfound sense of purpose and fulfillment. Witnessing the courage and strength of the children under our care has been a humbling reminder of the power of the human spirit to overcome adversity. Their unwavering determination to thrive despite the challenges they've faced has inspired me to approach life with a renewed sense of optimism and strength.

Amid the myriad of lessons learned and connections established at RISE, two virtues stand out as fundamental pillars of my journey: patience and tolerance. My time spent working with the children, staff, donors, sponsors, and volunteers has not only deepened my understanding of these virtues but has also transformed the way I navigate the world around me. Patience, I've discovered, is not merely a virtue but a dedicated practice of presence and understanding. I've come to appreciate the power of patience in fostering growth and healing and learning new processes. Whether it's guiding a child through moments of frustration and uncertainty or navigating through payroll and employee benefits in Mexico, patience has become an essential tool in my arsenal of caregiving and operations management. I'm constantly evolving in this aspect; there are moments when I notice strides in my patience. For instance, during a recent incident where one of the children was experiencing a raging episode, I was able to help her calm down by reassuring her of our love and support at the shelter. However, I also acknowledge instances where I falter, such as when I observed a staff teacher unprepared for a homework class causing me to lose my patience. It's a journey of growth and learning, and I recognize that I'm a work in progress.

My interactions with the dedicated staff and volunteers at RISE have also taught me invaluable lessons in tolerance, compassion, empathy, and the importance of community. Working alongside individuals from diverse backgrounds and walks of life has expanded my worldview and deepened my appreciation for the richness of human experience. We have shared moments of joy, laughter, and even tears. As you can imagine, some of the children at the shelter become very dear to us. When the time comes for them to leave—whether they are moving to an adolescent home, returning to a family member, or being adopted—we share many tears behind closed doors with each other, but then put on our happy faces to support the children as they move forward. We also share moments of fear together; for example, when we faced a hurricane this year, we didn't know what to expect. Despite our own fear, the director, my husband, and I reassured the children that everything would be okay. We worked together, sleeping on mattresses on the floor as water seeped into areas of the shelter, trees crashed around us, and electricity was lost. These experiences have built lifelong bonds and cherished friendships that will continue to shape my life for years to come.

One of the most rewarding aspects of my experience has been the opportunity to connect with the business and community leaders

Chapter 4

of Puerto Vallarta, as well as the vibrant community of entertainers who call this city home. Through my involvement with RISE, I've had the privilege of developing meaningful relationships with individuals who are not only passionate about making a difference but also possess the influence and resources to effect real change. One business we've formed a close relationship with stepped in to assist me in finding a potential cleaning person for the shelter. Surprisingly, a former employee needed a job, and not only did they refer her to us, but they also provided the funds to cover her salary and benefits! Additionally, during the talent show, one of our sponsors, a language school, generously offered scholarships for all our children to learn English at their institution. Even the local shoe repairmen generously fix the children's broken shoes free of charge.

The local food bank, known as Vallarta Cares, consistently lends us support in times of need. For instance, during the five days we were without power due to the hurricane, they provided us with a generator and helped clear the fallen trees from our courtyard. In return, we reciprocate by donating any excess food we receive that is nearing its expiration date. We are grateful and we are always on the lookout for opportunities to give back to those who assist us. During one summer, we received a donation of forty school desks exceeding our immediate needs. However, we were aware of a newly established non-profit school aimed at providing young girls with a better education and opportunities beyond traditional roles. Recognizing the potential impact, we delivered the donated desks to the school. As a result, one of our children now attends the non-profit Vallarta School for Girls and is thriving, benefiting from the challenges and opportunities it offers beyond those of the public school system. It's truly humbling to witness the unwavering support of the community, both in grand gestures and in the smallest acts of kindness.

These stories serve as consistent reminders to maintain an outward perspective. While our primary focus may be seeking support for the shelter, I've come to realize that by seeking opportunities to assist others, we inadvertently garner support for the shelter as well.

From local business owners who have generously supported our fundraising efforts to community leaders who have championed our cause, each connection has deepened our sense of belonging and commitment to the community we now call home. In fact, my connection with Influence Publishing and the opportunity to contribute to this book stem directly from my engagement with RISE. Julie Ann reached out to RISE to give back, and I am truly grateful for the connection!

Moreover, our collaboration with the talented entertainers of Puerto Vallarta has been nothing short of inspiring. Through events like our annual talent show, "So, You Think You Can RISE," we've had the opportunity to showcase the immense talent of our community while raising crucial funds for RISE Children's Shelter. In our most recent talent show, we recruited forty-nine business and individual sponsors and twenty-five professional entertainers. Many of these individuals and organizations are eager to support the community but may be too busy to seek out opportunities. Through our connections and events like the talent show, they not only gained increased visibility for themselves but also became aware of the children in need within their own community. By participating in the show, they were able to channel their efforts into supporting these children fostering a sense of connection and collective action toward a common cause.

But perhaps the most valuable part of my journey at RISE has been the friendships I've created along the way. Whether it's the camaraderie shared with fellow volunteers, the bond formed with the children we serve, or the connections made with business owners and community leaders, each relationship has left a permanent mark on my heart.

My time at RISE has taught me the true meaning of reciprocity—the acute interconnectedness of giving and receiving. While I may have set out to make a difference in the lives of the children at RISE, it is they who have ultimately changed me for the better. They have reminded me of the powerful impact that love, kindness, and compassion can have on the world around us. As a result, I've become more attuned to the impact of my actions on others, whether positive or negative. This heightened sensitivity has led me to continuously strive for awareness, seeking to make positive impacts on the people around me. By remaining mindful of how my words and deeds affect those in my life, I endeavour to cultivate a more compassionate and supportive environment for all. These recent years have only strengthened my innate inclination towards authenticity. I've always remained true to myself, never attempting to be someone I'm not. As I continue to embrace this authenticity in my new role as a volunteer, prioritizing empathy and determination, I find great solace in the knowledge that authenticity is a fulfilling way to live, regardless of the stage of life. While some may question why I dedicate myself to work so diligently in my retirement without financial compensation, I find fulfillment in other forms of reward. The satisfaction derived from making a meaningful difference in the lives of others far outweighs any monetary compensation.

In the end, my journey at RISE Children's Shelter is about more than just making a difference—it's been about building a community of compassion, resilience, and hope.

As I continue on this journey, I carry with me the memories of the connections I've made, the friendships I've created, and the countless moments of joy and laughter that have illuminated my path. And while my work at RISE may have started as a simple desire to give back, it has blossomed into a lifelong commitment to serving others and building a better world for all.

Conclusion: Discovering Personal Growth Through Service to Others

Our commitment to RISE Children's Shelter is unwavering, fueled by a simple yet deep belief: every child deserves a fair chance in life. These children, who have endured unimaginable hardships through no fault of their own, deserve to be heard, supported, and uplifted. Every action we take, every effort we make, is dedicated to ensuring that they receive the love, care, and opportunities they so rightfully deserve. As we strive to amplify their voices and share their stories with the world, we hope to inspire change and foster a future where all children, regardless of their circumstances, can thrive and flourish.

As I close this chapter on our journey with RISE Children's Shelter, I extend a heartfelt message to you. If you are seeking personal growth, fulfillment, and meaning in your own life, I invite you to consider the transformative power of helping others. My experiences at RISE have taught me that true fulfillment comes not from what we receive, but from what we give. Through acts of service, kindness, and compassion, I have discovered untapped reservoirs of strength, grit, and empathy within myself. I have witnessed firsthand the profound impact that a single act of kindness can have on the lives of others—and on our own.

So, if you find yourself searching for purpose or seeking a path to personal growth, I encourage you to reach out, lend a helping hand, and make a difference in the lives of those around you. Whether it's volunteering at a local shelter, mentoring a child in need, or simply offering a listening ear to someone in distress, know that every act of kindness has the power to spark transformation—both within yourself and in the world around you.

Chapter 4

In giving of ourselves, we receive far more than we could ever imagine. We discover the beauty of human connection, the fortitude of the human spirit, and the boundless capacity of the human heart to love and to heal.

May my journey inspire you to embark on your own path of service and self-discovery. And may you find, as I have, that the greatest rewards in life often come from the simplest acts of kindness.

About Lisa Manoogian

Lisa Manoogian currently is retired and helping manage and operate a children's shelter in Puerto Vallarta. Lisa is a Detroit native who migrated to Denver during high school years with her family before graduating from university in 1980. Her career began at Lockheed Missiles and Space where she transitioned from programming to software sales and management with many of the booming Silicon Valley start-up companies in that era. Embracing spontaneity, she earned the moniker of the "accidental executive" leading her to vibrant cities like San Francisco, Seattle, Los Angeles, and Chicago. She worked on innovative projects at the American Medical Association before retiring in 2018. Her biggest rewards are lasting connections forged with individuals across the country, cherishing the meaningful relationships cultivated through shared experiences and mutual respect. These connections remain the true joys of her life, serving as a testament to the power of genuine human connection.

lisa@risepv.com

5

My Bullies and Me: How Bullies Supported Me in Finding My Strength

By Anne Lindyberg

What is to give light must endure burning.

— **Victor Frankl,** *Man's Search for Meaning*

My Bullies and Me: How Bullies Supported Me in Finding My Strength

By Anne Lindyberg

I started to experience bullying by my peers at perhaps the age of three. There was a neighbour child who was about a half year younger than me; let's call her Honey.

Honey and I began playing together after the departure of my best friend to that point, Mikey. Mikey was also about six months younger than me, and we were very attached. We even got married one summer. My mother helped me assemble a suitable dress and veil out of the dress up bin, Mikey gave me some flowers, and the deed was done. We were so in love!

Within weeks, it seemed, his family moved away. Far enough away that that was the end of our marriage, and indeed, all acquaintance. I grieved! It's not just that I loved Mikey so much (I did), but also, he was an extraordinary playmate.

When the dust settled, perhaps a day or two after Mikey's departure, my mother pointed out that Honey was available in the neighbourhood, and maybe I would like to play with her. Well, what's a preschooler to do? One gets bored staying by mother's side all day. I gave it a shot.

Almost immediately there were challenges. What I remember may be formed from stories told later, although I do have a sense of the energy between Honey and I being difficult.

Honey would take my toys, and I would refuse to demand or take them back.

That a child between two and four would sometimes simply take the toys of another child isn't in and of itself surprising. But since I was around the same age, and this was so patently not the dynamic I experienced with my other friends, I was befuddled. I complained to Honey's mother when we were at her house. Didn't seem to help.

I complained to my own mother. Eventually my conversations with my mother went like this:

"Honey took my toy."

"Then take it back."

"Honey hit me."

"Then hit her back."

I simply could not do it. Even I could not understand why. "Is she bigger than you?" my mother would ask.

"No."

Chapter 5

"Then how can she hurt you?"

I could not explain it. I just knew I could not fight back. I was afraid, certainly, but it was more than fear. It felt as though my arms didn't work that way.

Over time, my relationship with Honey mellowed. We became more like two typical little girls playing Barbies and having ordinary squabbles that were resolved fairly. My family moved to a house two streets over, then her family moved further away, but near where we vacationed. Then her parents divorced, and her father moved far away.

We lost touch as friends when we were about eleven. Our families still have some contact—even today—but the few times over the years I've had the chance to talk with Honey, it's evident she doesn't desire communication with me. I really don't know why.

I have to say that Honey is someone I have always regarded as my first bully. With my understanding of developmental psychology and attachment, I bear her no ill will. Three-year-olds are some of the most authentic individuals on the planet, and Honey was no exception. She simply helped kick off my awareness of a pattern that would repeat itself and change the course of my life many times.

* * *

So what of the other bullies? Well, kindergarten was the next place. It was always certain kids—the kids who seemed, to me, grumpy and cranky. It was my habit to attempt to avoid them, but often they didn't avoid me. They might feign friendship in order to get me alone, then when we were alone, begin saying threatening things.

It was terrifying to think that I couldn't foresee this and avoid this, but that is exactly how it was. Complaining to teachers and my mother produced more "why don't you just stand up for yourself?" advice. Good question! I'd already asked myself that. Ultimately, I got the feeling that my challenges were burdensome to them. And that they were disappointed in me. I was failing at life, in the eyes of my parents and teachers, in kindergarten.

While it was true that other children experienced bullying in my class, I got it more than almost anyone. Over the course of elementary school, it began to feel like something was deeply wrong with me.

The bullying continued perhaps on a weekly basis throughout elementary school, ebbing at times when my friendship group was more solid. I got my first boyfriend in fifth grade, Don, and we stayed in a rather chaste yet emotionally satisfying "relationship"—much like my marriage to Mikey—for almost two years. This was probably the point at which I had the least trouble with bullies. I began to think I was done with them.

Seventh grade brought junior high. The sixth graders from four elementary schools were dispersed into a large and imposing building, exceeded in size and fearsomeness only by the high school. Due to an unfortunate educational decision made by my parents and sixth grade teacher during a meeting I was not invited to, the norm for that time and place, I was separated from all my elementary school friends. It was almost as though I'd started a new school.

Aside from the constancy of Girl Scouts, the weekly slog that was Catechism Class, and the presence of my good friend Gail who lived next door, it was as though my friends were gone.

In their place, in the rest of my classes, mostly unknown faces. A few classmates from my elementary school whom I liked, but none of my friends. There was one very scary boy who I was sure was going to end up killing someone. Slowly the bullies began to reemerge.

Seventh grade was difficult. Eighth grade was worse. By late fall,

Chapter 5

my bullies were showing up in teams of two or three. Girls mostly. And physical contact began as well with the goal being to humiliate. My parents had already refused the support of the guidance counsellor, so I was left to look after myself. By late winter, in the worst incident ever, the grandchild of the Phys. Ed. teacher was the ringleader of a group of no fewer than eight girls who had cornered me in the girl's shower, *Carrie* style. Mercifully we were all fully clothed. We were found by the aforementioned grandmother/Phys. Ed. teacher, and the crowd dispersed before any of the angry mob's kicks had done me any damage.

With this incident, I was finally believed, and I found myself in the guidance counsellor's office with three other classmates—girls I wasn't particularly friends with, but we had nothing against each other. It turns out I wasn't the only one being bullied, although it seems I had received the worst of it. A loose alliance was formed between the victims, with the support of the counsellor and administration as part of a plan to ensure greater safety. I don't recall it being particularly effective. Kind of a dismal collaboration lacking in empowerment.

I'd had enough. Something had to change. For a few years my mother had been threatening me with the local Catholic school if I didn't begin earning the grades she felt me capable of. "We'll send you to Bishop Gibbons!"

In a turn-the-tables moment in late eighth grade, I said to my mother, "Tell me about this Bishop Gibbons."

My timing was good. By this time my parents had had meetings with the principal, several teachers, perhaps even the dreaded school counsellor again. I think they were beginning to accept that circumstances were not likely to improve for me at the public junior high.

I took an entrance exam, and in the fall began my ninth-grade year at Notre Dame-Bishop Gibbons High School. I was a new student again among most who knew each other, the local Catholic grammar schools being feeders for NDBG. But I was told I would be safer; that "the compassion foundational to a Catholic school" didn't allow for the type of bullying I'd been experiencing.

This turned out to be largely true, although not for the reason stated. I suspect it was due to the influence of a chaplain who was locally well-known and regarded for both his compassion and influence, Father Paul Roman. He was not the principal, but he exuded an almost Albus Dumbledore-like quality of safety, which I now recognize as emotional maturity. Much later, I later learned that NDBG was also the receiving ground for students who had been expelled from their local public schools for many varieties of unacceptable behaviour. I always felt safe with Father Roman in the school.

All began reasonably well, except for two girls who began harassing me using almost the same tactics I'd experienced in junior high. I suppose the experience of confronting large groups of girls gave me a bit of courage, because for the first time I fought back. Not just one but both girls together.

It was late September of my ninth-grade year. I remember being so angry that this was happening *again*, after all I'd been through. During Phys. Ed. class (*Why* is it always Phys. Ed. class?), when their taunts and physical intimidation got to be too much, I pushed one away from me, and punched the other in the mouth. I was as shocked as the bullies and onlookers. The recipient of the punch got a swollen lip and a bit of blood on her teeth.

For this I received two detentions. I was horrified at first. Two detentions in my first month of school! I'd intended to complete four years without any, which I knew was my parents' expectation. But both my bullies got suspended for a day, and their parents had to come in for a conference. Mine were only called. The nuance wasn't lost on me. And while my parents treated it as shameful that I had

Chapter 5

detention, they didn't take it further. I imagine they wished I hadn't waited until high school to hit someone—or my mother at least. In any case, I must've done the right thing.

No bully ever bothered me in high school after that. Plus, a couple of girls who were apparently paying attention to the situation from afar adopted me into their friend group, saying I was very brave. This was new.

Work, marriage, children, divorce and two degrees followed. Many challenges and a fair amount of pain. My co-creations with my fellow humans, with certain exceptions, largely felt fair.

I thought I was done with bullies. Then, at the age of forty-three, I joined the ranks of New York State employees.

* * *

Five years out of grad school with my provisional certification as a school psychologist in New York State, and some related field experience providing counselling to individuals with developmental I was hired into a facility for boys. It was called the Industry Residential Center, so named for the Industry School, one of those sad rehabilitative schools built in the nineteenth century. It was a good opportunity for me as a school psychologist with a stronger interest in mental health than straight cognitive assessment and learning disabilities. I was thrilled to have been hired into the position.

All of the boys, aged eleven to twenty, had some form of adjudication, meaning they were legally ordered to be there. The facility was divided into two parts based on the boys' legal status. The boys in the limited-secure side were a bit younger with only juvenile delinquent status. Those in the secure centre were convicted of more serious crimes, up to and including murder.

I was initially placed on a team in the limited-secure facility. Each team—there were three—oversaw the housing, education, and treatment of a "cottage" of around thirty boys. It consisted of a cottage leader, two assistant cottage leaders, and around twenty uniformed staff who looked like guards and had similar duties, but also functioned more as personal support for the boys.

Each team was assigned a mental health professional who completed an intake assessment for each new arrival and coordinated mental health treatment for each resident in their cottage. This was my role, and my friend Leslie's in one of the other cottages.

This was a taxing assignment in many ways, yet I was happy to be there. The salary was higher than at the nonprofit where I'd been working and included good benefits and a generous retirement package. I was getting nearer to working with the population I always wanted to: kids with challenges related to attachment, poverty, discrimination, and the like.

It was a challenge learning the ways of a new system, integrating the requirements, while still bringing support and authenticity to my young clients and those colleagues who were appreciative.

Knowing what I know now, a residential treatment school runs like a prison—a system designed both *by* and *for* individuals experiencing challenges in their relationship with fear. I should have expected any unfinished business with bullies to come to the surface.

Originally the challenges of a new job presented themselves as expected. I experienced a little bit of discomfort in my interactions with colleagues and coworkers, and my new clients were already testing me. I anticipated this based on my past employment experiences and what I knew and had been told about the environment I was working in.

There was one individual whose approach as a bully was so direct, so unapologetic, that first witnessing her behaviour took my breath away. It was a coworker by the name of Lorena.

Chapter 5

The first thing I noticed was that Lorena was decidedly cool toward me. The staff in the facility, including mental health staff, were mostly male. In those early days there were times we were the only women at a meeting of six to ten staff. Her behaviour to me was both covertly and overtly hostile.

Suddenly, I had the feeling of being in the presence of a powerful enemy—even while a different part of me protested: "Powerful? I have more education. I'm at a significantly higher pay grade. Why am I so afraid of her?"

I could not explain it. I was as ashamed as I was scared. What I wasn't, yet, was angry. I can only suppose that being so new to the job, wanting to make a good impression, but most importantly not wanting to be fired, I had packed away my anger as thoroughly as I had as a child. It was nowhere to be found. Only fear. An unanswerable abyss of gaping, threatening fear.

Lorena made the most of it. She took every opportunity to snub me in meetings. She rolled her eyes. She made snide remarks. She didn't mind doing this publicly, but she saved her most scathing slights for when no one was watching.

To make matters even more infuriating (although now I simply think of it as interesting, even amusing), Lorena was an accomplished flirt with the male staff. She was well-respected and liked by them. One of my male colleagues, a fellow assistant cottage leader at Lorena's same pay grade, had worked with her longer and was aware of the vulnerabilities her openness with him seemed to create. On the other hand, he seemed incapable of noticing any of her negative behaviour.

The flirtation and sexual undertone in the facility was, for me, exceeded only by experiences I had during my time spent in the entertainment industry. It was not overt; I never found myself feeling truly harassed. It was simply a constant strain. There were multiple relationships between staff, even between management and hourly staff, some involving infidelity to partners who were never on campus. Razor wire-encased workplaces really do discourage your spouse from dropping by the office.

The first year of employment with New York State in a union position is probationary. I managed to get through that year and was recommended for permanency status, which was awarded in due course. This was a great relief because it meant that for the remainder of my tenure at the state, in whatever union position I held, at the same grade or lower, it would be next to impossible for me to get fired. This has some legitimate advantages, and some very specific and impactful disadvantages. One of which was that, among those with a permanent union position, which included everyone from a cottage leader on down, it was possible to be an absolute monster with little to no repercussions.

It seems Lorena understood this well. Her regular snide remarks, refusing to acknowledge when I was speaking to her (my polite, reasonable, business-related requests), and refusing to answer emails, all began to lead to anxiety in me that simply went up and up. My self-care strategies were pushed to the max, and it seemed like it could never have been enough. I used to be silently grateful that I had quit drinking alcohol entirely during that time, or I might've created quite a problem for myself.

One day, a few weeks after I'd received my permanent appointment, Lorena and I came across each other in the large, central, cavernous hallway of the main building. Unnaturally deserted, I was on my guard. I needed to walk past her. Having no need to talk with her, I simply made to walk past, giving a polite nod of greeting that could be easily ignored.

I don't remember what she said. What I do remember is that it was laden with contempt and possibly accusations of not doing my job.

Chapter 5

I looked at Lorena. I knew we were quite alone. She exuded a sense of physical power, but I was definitely taller.

I have a decent command of the English language, if no others. And like most with this skill, I can use it to hurt. I avoid doing this purposely. I didn't and don't enjoy fights that seem not to have a worthy purpose, that seek simply to hurt, humiliate or "otherize" people. And I am not in alignment with "punching down." Lorena was clever, certainly, but she had no idea what was about to hit her. It wasn't going to be fair, but she had been indifferent to my pain for so long—perhaps even relished it—I'd had enough.

It was the second time I'd punched the bully. This time I used words. My attack was personal, scathing, my voice three times as biting and contemptuous as hers. The words came from a dark place inside of me, which seemed to have been waiting for a moment such as this. With my second sentence I watched her eyes open in surprise and retreat. She wasn't expecting this.

After about five sentences, I forced myself to stop. Lorena had been mute from her first attempt to reply. I turned purposefully, my feet covering the distance back to my office like they were part of the cold, institutional floor. It was time to go home.

I'd like to relay what I said, but honestly, I cannot remember. I know I'm not proud of it. I dislike the idea of hurting another. I would've gotten away from Lorena if I could've; making a different choice is always my preference. Unfortunately, it was not possible. In reflection, it was not possible for Lorena to get away from me either. We were both prisoners of system we had agreed to join.

Work did not get easier. Within a couple of weeks, the director approached me and asked me to change to the secure centre team, to replace a retiring colleague. I would be the only mental health provider on that campus, but it was right next door to the limited secure centre, and my colleagues were only an email or phone call away. I gratefully accepted.

I never had the slightest trouble with Lorena again. I did learn, much later, that her behaviour toward my friend Leslie worsened after my departure. Leslie had been hired a couple of months after I was, and she left for her job in an adult prison a few weeks before I left for a different agency, because the secure centre closed. Leslie remains one of my good friends and favourite people, with the loving heart of a dedicated therapist.

This situation having gone on for a full year, I had a lot of time to think about it. About bullies. Bullying. About myself, feeling like a victim again, of petty, schoolroom slights, after all these years.

In the end I think what happened is that after I gained permanency, I began to allow myself to feel angry again. It didn't happen suddenly. And I want to be clear, I am not in alignment with blame and rage as strategies for living. I never have been. To be sure, they have their place, but I do not wish to live in a situation where I must use them, or they are used on me.

In fact, I've come to understand the difference between anger and blame, and the proper role of anger, in a quite nuanced and useful way since that time.

In my experience, anger is the emotion that arises when we want to say "No, thank you!" or "No more!" or "That does not fit for me!" with sufficient emphasis, seeming to be required, to assert our own right to influence the direction of a co-creative interaction.

Anger doesn't typically need to come up at the family-style dinner table when we want to pass on the green bean casserole: a simple pass, or gentle "no, thank you" will do. But what about when someone pushes something on us? *Insisting* that we take some of that casserole that we know we will be unable to choke down, or might even harm us in a way the insister does not understand (as with food sensitivities)?

Chapter 5

When someone is asserting the expectation, even the right, to dictate without any input from another how a co-creative interaction will go: this is when an individual really benefits from a healthy relationship with their own anger.

I didn't quite have one at the time, but it was coming.

* * *

It has been more than a decade since my time at the Industry School. I have experienced significant challenges and upheavals since then. In many ways, it feels like I have put my vulnerability to bullies to bed.

It is true: if we are being treated disrespectfully, we must respond. We must object. That might involve "hitting back."

Perhaps the more important lesson, however, is that we must have a place of safety from which to do that. We must feel supported. As children, we must have supportive family and/or friendship community. As adults, we must find that strength within ourselves. The strength to say, in whatever words work, "This is not how I will accept being treated."

My perspectives on the experiences of my life continue to deepen. Sometimes I think this is what John Denver meant when he sang "It turns me on to think of growing old."

It has taken this long, as I approach the age of sixty, to realize that the bullies were me, and I was them. Attracted to each other by the fact that we were both desperately afraid, and in our different ways, trying to put a brave face on it.

I wouldn't attempt to rush anyone to this understanding, though. It is the richer for the journey I travelled to discover this oasis of camaraderie, love, and appreciation for those with whom I share my life. My mother has enjoyed telling people when asked what I was like as a young child, "She was always wanting to do things by herself. I would try to help her get dressed, or some other thing, she would pull away saying 'No, Mommy, I do by self!'" I'm still that child.

I don't need to do everything by myself any longer, though. At long last, and with the help of my most memorable nemeses, I'm facing the fear of my own vulnerability. Or I'm beginning to. And moving in greater synchrony and harmony with my fellow beings, to our improved mutual enjoyment. It was a long time coming, and sweeter for the wait.

When I consider what I might've wanted and benefitted from in my younger years from those in caregiving, teaching, then leadership roles, I realize a couple of things.

Firstly, that bullying is going to exist as long as there are people rejecting aspects of themselves. Rejecting aspects of self or community can both be necessary at times and also an impediment to being more fully human, which makes it kind of a paradox. The thing about pushing experiences or perspectives aside because someone decides they cannot be dealt with at present is that those experiences or perspectives must be reclaimed for the possibility of wholeness to reemerge. They are not disembodied: experiences and perspectives are by necessity attached to a person. If we have decided that an experience or perspective cannot be tolerated in a given situation—and sometimes this decision must be made, by each of us in turn—we cannot refuse to return to what we banished without feeling pain as visceral as if we had to amputate a limb to save our own life. We are not just our own bodies: we are each other as well. In fact, we are everything we see, hear, smell, taste, touch, and more. Our true nature is too vast for us to comprehend.

And this leads to my second realization. If the scope of our challenges is truly too vast to comprehend, what is the best approach? What approach empowers each person with the feeling of support and love that leads to the courage to share their gifts freely, without fear of the inevitable rejections that are part of our world?

Begin with oneself. Every morning presents a new beginning. When we awaken into the body, we can notice it. Appreciate the presence of each part of our body, validate our experience of physical limitation or pain. Having done so, we can expand our experience of self to our personal space, engaging with that space, with full appreciation for every item placed or strewn in our home. When we are ready to leave our bedroom or home and engage with the world, we bring our full, embodied selves.

The embodied self, the individual who feels supported, cannot be bullied, nor can they bully.

For those who are tasked with caring for or teaching children, or facilitating teams in the workplace or community, when bullying comes to your attention, realize that you are intimately involved simply by witnessing or knowing of it. Your observation is not an accident. What we see, we are meant to see. And if we witness one individual attempting to victimize another, at any age, in any circumstance, we must connect with our feelings and allow ourselves to feel what our bodies bring us in that circumstance. Having done this, perhaps we will think it appropriate to check in with our values and ask, "Is this in my alignment?" This is the approach that will lead to embodied action, and ultimately, the healing of the communities where bullying and victimizing occurs.

There is no behavioural blueprint beyond being present with oneself as fully as possible. The conflict is not solely between bully and victim: it is the epicentre of the transformation birthing itself within each individual and within the community. And there is no need to worry about getting it wrong, because it will recur until we fully allow it.

About Anne Lindyberg

Anne Lindyberg is a licensed mental health counsellor and licensed clinical professional counsellor in private practice in Cedar Rapids, Iowa, U.S., serving clients in person and through telehealth in Iowa, and residents of Illinois through telehealth. She employs Satir Transformational Systemic Therapy and Deep Brain Reorienting in her practice, providing support for those reclaiming their wholeness and healing their attachment wounds. She can be found online through the website for her practice, the Midwest Center for Transformational Change PLC, and on YouTube at the link below. A graduate of the College of Saint Rose in Albany, New York, Anne is a New York State certified school psychologist as well.

www.mwcftc.com
www.youtube.com/@AnneLindyberg

6

Heartbreak: Our Catalyst for Authenticity and Legacy

By Dionne Eleanor

They say one of the hardest things in life is grieving the loss of someone who is still alive.
I believe this does not only apply to our interpersonal intimate connections, but to ourselves.
That feeling that "something doesn't feel right" that many people have is often a subtle grieving.
A warning from their nervous system that they are losing a bit more of themselves every day that they continue to carry unresolved heartbreak.

— **Dionne Eleanor**

Heartbreak: Our Catalyst for Authenticity and Legacy

By Dionne Eleanor

We are not meant to deal with heartbreak alone, yet many of us struggle silently behind closed doors trying to comprehend the best step forward. We come from an ancestral line full of amazing voices and talents, many unheard, unseen, and silenced from pain, compounded heartbreak, and a lack of tools to process.

Although it is common knowledge, it's worth highlighting that we aren't born with insecurities, identity issues, or heartbreak—we adopt or learn them. Humanity has come a long way, but I believe there is still a lot of opportunity to expand global knowledge, skill, and confidence on heartbreak—authentically.

Perhaps your life is okay but you're the type of person that wants an outstanding life. I intend to use my personal and professional experience to share authentic insights on this taboo yet very human subject of heartbreak. As you read some of my journey, I hope you feel empowered to step into your authenticity and start taking solid steps forward to turn your losses into legacy today.

Growing Up

Although I do believe we are all equal, it cannot be denied that my ancestral path and family have experienced tumultuous heartbreak that was heavily connected to their ethnicity and place of birth. This heartbreak is perhaps a little more complex as my heritage is mixed.

Once upon a time when I was a child, like you, I could not fully articulate my experiences, thoughts, and emotions to others. I did not have the language skills to express my emotions verbally as a baby. Once I had learned how to speak, it was still difficult to communicate my emotions and feelings for many years. I discovered that I was born into a family where "talking back" was considered disobedient and disrespectful behaviour. Adversity was the norm, and working hard was praised. Attaining an abundance of wealth with ease created suspicion and gossip. Respect for elders and authority figures is often deeply ingrained in Afro-Caribbean and Indian culture; I was blessed to be born as a second-generation immigrant in the United Kingdom (UK) into a family with a dominant lineage of these cultures. My late father's bloodline was Barbados, Native Indian and my mother's was Jamaican, German and Welsh.

Growing up, I witnessed family members dying young, often before the age of fifty-five. Despite all of this, we didn't talk about the pain we felt, the grief, or anything else that challenged us emotionally. We didn't talk about the pain we felt from losing and rejecting parts of our cultural identity to fit into the local culture of the UK. We didn't talk about the racism, sexualization, and financial hardship we experienced.

Chapter 6

My Grandmother on my mother's side was one of five hundred migrants from Jamaica that the British Empire brought to the UK in 1948 to help rebuild the country after World War II. She was sixteen, a high achiever academically, and had left her family behind on a beautiful tropical beached country that now many pay thousands of dollars to visit on vacation. She was promised the chance to have a better life with citizenship, higher education, and better long-term financial stability than she could if she stayed in Jamaica.

The reality was that she was invited to help address labour shortages and help rebuild a mess that she never created. She met racism, prejudice, discrimination, and challenges over working long hours. She experienced being wrongly denied access to healthcare, housing, pensions, and other essential services. Changes in immigration laws and policies over the years, coupled with inadequate documentation and record-keeping, resulted in some people being wrongfully detained, denied access to public services, or threatened with deportation.

At times my grandmother felt treated like an "undesirable" foreigner, despite having lived and worked in and for the UK for years. We didn't talk about that.

You see my grandmother was not a talker, especially about pain and heartbreak. There was no time or purpose for that, and even if she did consider speaking to a therapist, that would have been another stigma or an indicator that something about her was "incorrect."

It is no surprise that I was born to a mother who also was not a talker. My mother was born as a middle child, and my grandmother was a single parent to her and her six siblings for much of their childhood. My late grandfather was a wonderful man in many ways, but struggled to articulate his emotions. He sadly gambled his grief and trauma away, before later in life developing dementia and passing away.

On my father's side, my grandmother passed away at fifty-four years old. I will never forget the hair-raising scream my cousin released in the church at my grandmother's funeral. I didn't know much about her, besides that she was adopted as a child, had a mixed heritage, and never knew her parents. It's interesting how, as a child, you see things as just "the norm." Looking back now I am shocked that at the tender young age of fifty-four, my grandmother had lost most of her hair and one of her legs. Her husband, my dad's father and my grandad, had lost almost all of his teeth. I still remember playing with his dentures as a child, taking them in and out of the glass of water. As an adult now who works in the well-being industry, I look back and feel my grandparents had a rather short life.

My only surviving grandparent is my mother's mum, Joyce, selected to move to the UK as part of the HMT Windrush generation. Interestingly I am compared to her a lot by family members and close family friends. Some say I am more like my grandmother than my mother, especially concerning resilience and adaptability to new environments. My life has been punctuated by multiple painful heartbreaks. Each heartbreak created a mark on my spirit and shaped the course of my life in the direction of desiring to become deeply knowledgeable on the subject areas I was suffering with. It was a blessing to be born into a family that prided education and wisdom highly.

Who I Have Become Today

I was born into a family haunted by the shadows of ancestral trauma and personal hardship. Yet, it was precisely these challenges that fuelled my determination to forge a new path for myself.

I am the founder of The Body Sage™—a movement of positive education around heartbreak, grief, and pain recovery. It's my mission to bring lightness, ease, normality, clarity, and intention to these normal yet difficult subjects that people globally struggle to resolve. Subjects that I and my own family struggled to resolve in the past. I aim to expand global knowledge on the body and psychosomatic sickness and pain that is rooted in compounded heartbreak, past trauma, and sexual violation. The Body Sage™ method is a unique combination of somatics, voicework, sound therapeutics, Rapid Transformation Therapy (RTT) hypnosis, spinal flow therapy, meditation, ceremony, tantric philosophy, and action-based empowerment mentoring. The intention is to liberate people from their past, including that which is ancestral, and to give them the skills to fulfill their dreams. The name Body Sage came to me in a dream in 2020 following a deep heart-focused meditation. At the time, I was marketing myself under the name Embrace Living Now which felt okay, but not specific enough for what I felt coming through to share with the world. In that meditation, I sought guidance on a brand name that would communicate the concept of body wisdom.

In 2019, I took my life to a new level by emigrating to Mexico. I had no savings, partner, job, residency, or home lined up and could not speak Spanish. However, I was crystal clear that it was time to launch a new version of myself and create something that would positively impact the world. Fast forward to today, my life has done a 360, and I have obtained all that I never had before arriving.

> *The truth is we all, including you, have the power to rewrite our narrative and create the life we desire. Sometimes it's simply a case of remembering who we truly are, and from there we can start to access the "how."*
>
> —Dionne Eleanor

The Catalyst for My Authentic Legacy Creation: Heartbreak

I see heartbreak as a human response to the loss of something that matters. Often the real heartbreak that creates the most grief is a person's loss of authentic self: living day-to-day, not feeling like this is the life they deserve to live, and not knowing how to reclaim that authentic self. It's a slow erosion and can chip away at self-esteem. Heartbreak inevitably harms a person's physical and mental health when there is a lack of tools, resources, and support.

The "heartbreak compound effect" is a term that I created based on the premise that over time, if left unresolved, heartbreak gets compounded no matter how big or small it may have initially been. If left unaddressed, this compounded heartbreak can result in disastrous circumstances. The death of my father, the severe illness of my mother, my broken spine, and having survived sexual assault were some of my most prominent painful initiations into this work.

My father died suddenly, shortly after his fiftieth birthday. The diagnostic report said it was a heart attack, but my father had never had any heart issues previously, nor was there a history of heart attacks in his lineage. He did, however, experience multiple heartbreaks, and as a first-generation immigrant black male, he felt multiple pressures to perform and be whatever people wanted him to be.

When he died, it was difficult for me to process the pain. I didn't have the luxury of talking to my family about it and I didn't have the money for therapy of any sort. Throughout childhood, I learned to use my voice to sing and chant privately as a method to process heartbreak and pain. But this time with my father it felt different. It felt like I had lost a part of myself. Even though he had been emotionally absent and machismo at times, he was still my father and there was nothing more sacred than his love and the intensity of it. For seven years I pretended he was on vacation. It was necessary

Chapter 6

because when he died, my mother entered into a deep depression where she did not speak or eat.

As you read this, I'd like you to consider the reality that I was about twenty-two-years-old and had three brothers at the ages of seventeen, eleven, and ten, all with strong personalities. I was completing my Master's degree in a different city and working two jobs. I did not have extended family support; in fact, I had the opposite. I received hurls of emotional abuse from my emotionally-dysregulated aunts and uncles along with high expectations from my grandmother that, as the oldest sibling, it was my duty to fix and organize the chaos. I was thrown into learning how to be a parent to my mother and brothers, dealing with extended family politics, and trying to complete my education.

Pretending my father was on holiday was the perfect escape route for my broken heart to have a little bit of respite and it allowed me to delay my own heartbreak compound effect experience.

Despite the challenge, I completed my degree with distinction and several awards. However, it wasn't long before I witnessed a deeper heartbreak, perhaps one more painful—the loss of my true self. I was so busy being the parent, the fixer, and the pleaser to my family that I lost the sense of who I was and my true personal power. This became apparent to me when I found myself struggling to leave an emotionally abusive relationship shortly after completing my degree.

Heartbreak, compounded over time, has been shown in research over and over again to deeply impact an individual's sense of self and purpose, thus leading to a disconnection from their authenticity and life mission. In his paper "Heartbreak and Loss," psychologist George Bonanno from Colombia University shares that chronic stress resulting from the emotional pain of heartbreak can lead to dysregulation of the stress response system, affecting mood, cognition, behaviour, and thus a disconnection from personal authenticity.

Dr. Sonia Lupien also shared in her research article "The Effects of Chronic Stress on the Brain" that it's common for the cumulative effects of multiple heartbreaks to erode one's sense of self-worth, self-clarity, and sense of direction.

I remember speaking to one of my close friends on the telephone, as usual complaining about my abusive boyfriend. One day the conversation went differently. She said, "Dionne, I can't talk to you about him anymore unless it's to do with you leaving him." I was shocked. I felt I didn't have a clear roadmap to move forward. Although it felt harsh and uncomfortable, the boundary set by my friend propelled me into a key shift toward healing and regaining my authenticity.

Deep down inside I knew that my life would lack purpose if I did not start living authentically.

My Journey to Motivation, Clarity, and Healing

So how did my personal experience with heartbreak motivate me to obtain what some may consider ambitious goals? How did I step into my authenticity despite heartbreak?

Throughout my life, my commitment to self-education and vulnerability in sharing my story with at least one trusted person remained steadfast. These were integral things that gave me an edge to turn my heartbreak into a legacy. My education also often allowed me to have periods of introspection. The intensity of my emotions, whether anger, sadness, or hope, led me to these paths of introspection, and from there I connected with a high-quality education.

I must also celebrate my grandmother and her sacrifice at a young age, as it allowed me to be born as a British citizen. With its strong developed infrastructure and fairly stable economy, the UK blessed me with a powerful passport, good education, scholarships, and healthcare.

I travelled a lot for many years, but always returned to the UK to perform my "duties" as the eldest child and daughter. I moved to Mexico to lower my outgoing expenses, increase my quality of life, and get some rest as I was heading towards medical burnout in the UK. Mexico has also allowed me to go deeper into my heartbreak wounds and release fragments of co-dependency and unnecessary guilt.

My move to Mexico was not intentional; I was invited by my friend on vacation and ended up getting headhunted by a retreat centre and staying. I wanted to make friends authentically, so I created a digital poster for breathwork and meditation at a local beach by donation. I knew this would be a better way for me to meet likeminded souls without going out in the late evening. The word got around in the local community and soon after I was approached by a leading retreat centre to coordinate and host their retreats.

I soon realized I had landed my dream job—it was amazing! Despite this, choosing to live in Mexico was a complex dilemma for my heart. The UK was easy and comfortable, I could sort of live authentically, but not fully. Mexico was incredible, but I needed to learn so many things: the language, how the healthcare system worked, how to negotiate and create work opportunities, how to make friends, the rental market, and more. I spent many nights crying, feeling lonely, and feeling physical discomfort in my body. I had to go deeper and heal the part of me that did not want to step fully into her authentic life. I had no desire to live permanently in the UK. I realized living in the UK did not allow me to express my authentic self. It broke my heart to know that many of my loved ones lived there or nearby.

After staying in Mexico for just over a year, I acquired the money to visit the UK. Fortunately, as part of this trip, I attended a live Tony Robbins convention called "Unleash the Power." It was life-changing! Attending Tony Robbins was a great opportunity to be in an immersive environment with people like me; thousands of people who have experienced a lot of adversity and desire to be the most authentic empowered version of themselves. This event opened my eyes and encouraged me to trust in my ability to make a conscious choice for Mexico to be my new home.

Since that day, I have committed to showing up, practicing self-care, and giving value to the community around me. Creating a nest to ground in, Mexico allowed me to reflect on my years of study, healing, and global client work. I identified patterns and incredible learning opportunities that help us to shift the global narrative on how we look at transmuting our heartbreak pain.

Turning Heartbreak into Authentic Legacy

To transform my heartbreak into an authentic legacy, I created a framework called The 7 Wise Bodies© to support the process. This framework was developed based on the premise that when healing heartbreak, different layers contribute to full authentic expression. One of my mentors, Marisa Peer, a renowned rapid transformational hypnotherapist, told me "When the eyes don't cry another part of the body weeps." When I heard this, I understood that moving through that pain, step-by-step with support, would bring true liberation and enable me to live a happy, authentic life.

As you read the descriptions below, recall the heartbreak of my father's death since the grief was challenging for me to shift. I have provided insight into what the layers felt like for me and I invite you to visualize me as a young woman, close to burnout, finally with the space and time to be deeply present with herself. Imagine now, as I prepare myself to see what my heartbreak has to say, that my body presents itself as a set of Russian dolls (starting from the exterior, working in). Each doll would represent a crucial area of my soul that I needed to work through to liberate myself from heartbreak, reclaim my authenticity, and find clarity to move forward.

1. The Grief Body
When my father passed away, I felt like I was enveloped in a viscous, clinging substance. It was coating my soul as a protective barrier from the harshness of the outside world. It was a sensation of sliminess, as if I was constantly trying to shake off its sticky residue only for it to ooze back. I didn't realize it then, but this was the layer others encountered when they first met me. The people who had known me for several years could see beyond this layer and not judge me negatively by it. I had to consistently integrate high-quality rest and therapeutics into my routine to heal my grief body layer. I had to be disciplined with my sleep-wake cycle and incorporate adaptogen herbs to nurture my nervous system. Things like lemon balm tea, cacao, rose, milk thistle, broths, ashwagandha, and Irish moss were staples.

2. The Flesh Body
Moving deeper, I encountered my flesh body layer. Here, I felt and noticed a tenderness in my being—physical wounds of my heartbreak. I experienced aches, pains, and physical illness as manifestations of this layer. I had stiffness in my thoracic spine and my right-side psoas muscle felt so tight that it could snap at any point. There was no thinking my way out of the discomfort and hiring a personal trainer, massage therapist, and chiropractor did not cut it either. I had to stop outsourcing the relationship to my flesh body and commit to an interdependent relationship with it and whichever practitioners I chose to trust, nourishing my body both topically and internally, and ensuring that I used non-toxic products on my skin and around my home. I had to communicate with practitioners where I felt discomfort and focus on letting go of the heartbreak I

knew lay at the root of my discomfort. I focused on physically balancing my heart, liver, spleen, kidneys, and adrenals using Chinese medicine meridian principles with my yin yoga practice.

3. The Breath Body

Through conscious breathwork, I connected with the life force coursing through my veins, regulating my nervous system and oxygenating every cell. Daily breathwork sessions of at least ten minutes allowed me to release stored trauma, bringing greater self-awareness and clarity to my inner landscape. Synchronizing breathwork with movement via the practice of kundalini yoga helped me master this layer. My predominant four breathwork practices consisted of bramani and nadhi shodna breath in the evenings, and kapalabahti and kumbhaka breath in the mornings, practicing this at least four times a week. The difference was astounding.

4. The Genius Body

Once I had spent some time nourishing my flesh body and accessing my breath body, I began to tap into the edge of my genius again. It literally felt like a lightbulb activated in my brain. I felt invigorated and more energetic in my days, and it would feel tempting to be overambitious with my time. Accessing my genius body meant I had to practice deep active listening: listening to myself and to others. I integrated non-negotiable solo time each week and took myself on dates. The fog of heartbreak really started to lift as I made time for myself this way. I felt like I was tapping into my highest self, a version of me with profound knowing and understanding. I felt like a delicious and juicy person emerging with clarity, grace, and purpose. I integrated a practice of reading daily, or if time was short, I would listen to a podcast or an audiobook. I looked at the pattern of books in my home and got rid of any books that pushed me deeply into thinking, and purchased books that inspired me to feel. Although I love the principle of digital books, I knew it was important at this time to have physical tools, so I indulged in purchasing hard copies of authors that tantalized my soul. Poets like Rumi and introspective writers like Yung Pueblo and Bell Hooks; writers who use so little with words to evoke much of what is felt and found in the heart.

5. The Spiritual Body

My genius body gave me a sense of intelligent confidence. It reminded me that people don't care what you do much of the time as long as it doesn't affect them negatively. Exploring my spiritual body layer, I investigated my belief systems about life and death. I asked myself what God and religion meant, and what I was drawn to and why. I committed to having a personal, private relationship with my own concept of creator, one that would not be confined or need to be upheld by others. I declared this by hosting my own private cacao ceremony at home and reading out self-commitment vows of transformation for myself. Included in these vows was a commitment to give my ancestors back their pains and commit to being the highest version of myself, standing in the name of love. I felt an inner radiance within me, and I felt like I expanded into the realm of infinite power, grace, and creation with clarity and intent. I remember feeling like people noticed me more and becoming incredibly magnetic. I felt like this layer was a huge game-changer for me in terms of personal authenticity. I stood in integrity with who I saw myself to be, committed to, and acknowledged with gratitude the support of that which was bigger than me. I felt like anything I desired would eventually come my way, especially because the desire would be sincere and with pure intention for the greater good.

6. The Sex Body

I worked on the prior body layers for about a year before choosing to safely reopen and activate my sexual body layer. Prior to this I had chosen to commit to conscious celibacy. I had opportunities to explore my sexuality on many occasions, but I did not feel I would be making a conscious choice. After a few unhealthy dating situations, I saw that I simply needed a bit of time to connect with myself first. I started to explore the wisdom of Tantra and relationships, studying with several of the world's leading teachers. Exploring Tantra and conscious relationships totally shifted gears for me. It was like I had put on a new pair of glasses and saw the world and my body in a whole new light. I learned the wisdom of sex magic, meditations, and rituals to connect to the earth and my body. This led me to feel orgasmic even without intercourse. I felt like I could call forth beautiful relationships and see my own beauty and I felt turned on by myself. This body layer reminded me of the sweet tender nature of love and connection. A big part of healing and re-empowering this layer of myself meant allowing myself to accept that I had lost loving relationships I had created with another.

7. The Voice Body

Finally my true voice—I found this deep, deep, deep inside, the deepest layer within my body. To explore this layer, I gathered with small groups of three to five people and engaged in an exchange of vocal expression with witnessing and active listening. These were people I found on Facebook in a group interested in music and sound, though none of us were professionally qualified in the field and had varying degrees of self-confidence. We met for around six months and called our time together "Voices Without Borders." It was a fantastic, powerful, simple practice allowing us each to clarify our own unique voice while being witnessed by others. Some people were there to get over a huge fear of public speaking, others had souls begging to belt out songs they had nowhere else to sing. Personally it was an opportunity for me to reconnect to that little girl version of me—the little girl who would sing privately to transmute her pain. It was an opportunity for her to be seen. What was remarkable was that allowing that part of me to be seen in this group dynamic transferred into my everyday life. I noticed I felt more confident in general conversation and my actions and words had greater alignment.

Exploring these bodies offered profound transformation into authenticity and continues to do so. Initially I felt shrouded in the dense fog of the first body layer, my grief body. I tried to shrug it off with self-deception and avoidance, but it didn't work. It was once I began to peel back that first layer and delve deeper, layer-by-layer, that I started to find my true self. I am so happy that I was able to reclaim my autonomy and authenticity. Now, I am paving my path towards sharing my lessons to support others in their healing, creating a legacy from the depths of my past sorrow.

My Commitment to Drive Global Change

Part of my mission with sharing knowledge through The Body Sage™ method is to keep things simple and relatable. It's for that reason that, whether I am processing my own heartbreak or working with clients, I usually map out the process in four simple steps:

1. understand the heartbreak;
2. agree on solutions to move forward;
3. implement new habits and behaviours with accountability; and
4. sustain and excel a new lifestyle.

The Healing Journey to Authenticity

The time it takes and the precise detail of each step are relative to the situation and weight of the heartbreak.

A key part of my life work is to challenge fixed belief systems about the way heartbreak is seen and dealt with. I passionately advocate the normality of heartbreak and I feel it's important to remind people that heartbreak can be felt from a wide range of sources. Nobody should feel alone or alienated in their pain. With understanding and guidance, I am confident that we can all have better governance over our heartbreak recovery and turn our pain into positive purpose. Over the next few years, I seek to take my work into universities and corporate offices as these are two hot places where people are developing themselves and have experienced their first "heartbreak" life events.

More people need to know what is their true "yes" and "no," and the rhythm and wisdom of their bodies. Saying things like "time will heal" creates a false sense of healing, and more internal mental noise, and is not a sustainable method for longevity, health, and nervous system regulation. We all know cognitively that intimate relationships can end, that money can ebb and flow, and that we are not immortal. However, it's a sad reality to know many people are living shorter more stressful lives because of a lack of resources on how to deal with these heartbreaks when they occur.

I feel fortunate that I saw my adversity in life as an initiation to access internal power to move forward. That perspective led me to authenticity, personal empowerment, and creating my methods to share with the world. I believe deeply that we all deserve to have the chance to get better at transmuting our heartbreak so we can live a happy authentic life despite our past pains.

Nothing and nobody have the right or power to steal our open heart; we are here to stand with a sense of joy, freedom, truth, and sovereignty. I hope that via my methods and living my own authentic life, I can support others to turn their losses into legacy and live authentically too.

About Dionne Eleanor

Dionne Eleanor, founder of The Body Sage method, is an experienced transformational empowerment mentor and therapist who has worked internationally for over fourteen years. She specializes in helping people transmute the pain of heartbreak, compounded grief, and relationship dysfunction so they can relaunch and revive their well-being, intimate connections, and businesses.

Dionne is an expert for Marriage.com and has also received awards for being a business leader. Her global Body Sage alumni and clients get fast results experiencing a unique blend of action-based empowerment mentoring, voice and sound therapy, movement therapeutics, somatic psychotherapy, Tantric philosophy, sacred ceremony and ritual, and scientific neuroplasticity training within Rapid Transformation Therapy (RTT).

Outside of her commitment to driving a positive shift with her clients globally, you will often find Dionne enjoying her yoga practice, ecstatic dance, cooking plant-based meals, and reading. You can learn more about Dionne and her offerings on her website and by connecting with her on Instagram.

www.thebodysagemethod.com
www.instagram.com/@dionneeleanor_

7

Nepal to Mexico: Adventures of Personal Truth and Human Connections

By Sky Gerlowski

The millions are awake enough for physical labor; but only one in a million is awake enough for effective intellectual exertion, only one in a hundred millions to a poetic or divine life. To be awake is to be alive.

— **Henry David Thoreau,** *Walden*

Nepal to Mexico: Adventures of Personal Truth and Human Connections

By Sky Gerlowski

Whatever you need will cross your path—a channelled message I received from a currently unknown entity that identified itself only as a spirit. And how right this spirit was! While I have usually relied on my own actions to obtain my goals and desires, I now hold firm to the belief that sometimes it comes down to the right person coming across your path at the right moment. With the gift of hindsight, I have learned that predetermined actions are not always enough to give you the perspective you need to achieve the best results, no matter what they are. Whether to be a comfort in times of crisis, a guide with loving intentionality, an opportunity for us to offer help, or merely there to behave in a way that provides a contrast to highlight what you don't want in your life, these individuals can provide insight to take you one step closer to knowing and receiving what you do want. Our interactions with those around us and the corresponding feelings they inspire are our greatest feedback in the physical realm and can be used as signs to direct us along our paths.

My expedition from viewing existence as an obligation to creating a genuinely miraculous life has taken two key things: the use of my free will to deliberately participate in my experience and connections with magical people whose relationships have helped me forge my path toward a life of joy, peace, and authenticity.

Wherever You Go, There You Are

As American professor Jon Kabat-Zinn says, "Wherever you go, there you are," meaning wherever you go mentally, physically, emotionally, or spiritually in any given moment, well, that is where you are in that moment. Luckily for us, every individual moment is an opportunity to use our free will to choose either the same circumstances or a path that redesigns our current reality. I have found the option of a new path to be the adventure that just keeps on adventuring. Sometimes the growth we experience is a slow and incremental integration toward our perceived ideal selves or life, and sometimes, it is a profound, instantaneous revelation or encounter that transforms your existence or understanding of it.

Whether or not we are receptive to it, life is simply a progression of personal development, growth, and conscious self-awareness. Personal authenticity, being in direct relation to this awareness of self, means that technically we are always being our authentic selves based on our current understanding and where we are in our personal evolution at that point in time. Everything we do, say, or be is a direct reflection of who we are in that exact moment. Remembering that people are dynamic and change is inevitable makes the concept of authenticity fluid.

As we speak of authenticity, what we are talking about is personal truth—the alignment of our participation in our lived experience with that which is true for us (regardless of what is true for others). Identifying personal truth sounds simple enough on the surface. However, when you consider that from the moment we are born, we are being influenced by stimuli from outside of ourselves, often with positive intentions from those who genuinely care and have accepted these ideas as their truth. Religion, law, government mandates, medical advice, school systems, parental perceptions, and corporate marketing are some examples of things we are encouraged to welcome as truth. As our human instinct is to be accepted, and these influences are all we have experienced (so far), acceptance of these concepts as truth is often inevitable. Even though they are hardly ever for our highest good, as these ideas aid the creation of our core beliefs, they set the parameters in which we live our lives, limiting our potential through our "need" to assimilate. My current awareness of my authenticity, after much consideration and inner questioning of who I am and what I'm doing here, appears to be the quest for personal change, clearing out enough worry, fear, reactionary responses, habitual loops, limiting beliefs, and general garbage to be able to identify and follow that which brings me joy. It was in Mexico at the end of my twenties that this really began, and I realized that without the nuance of pondering my personal truth, deliberately constructing my value system and intentional connections, and deciphering my feelings and emotions, I was simply alive just because I was alive and dealing with it.

I focused my attention inward to assess myself and my place in the world and revealed an almost devastating contrast between the connection and enjoyment I had with life and how I would ultimately prefer to perceive my experience. It occurred to me that I didn't know how to have fun, or how to perceive joy in a way that was, in fact, joyful. Years prior, I had been a mere product of my environment; partying, drinking, dancing, up until sunrise and beyond, gossiping, smoking, buying a new outfit for each event, heels every day, make-up on all occasions, working to spend the majority of my money on vacations, vices and what those around me had decided was a "good time." There were indeed enough people in the same position all considering these behaviours fun, so there I was, in the name of fun, participating. There had to be more to it; surely the point of life wasn't to have enough free time and disposable income for vacations, parties, and drinking on the beach.

Although I was consistently rewarded at work for my ability to build rapport with clients, I felt that I was unable to have a meaningful conversation on a personal level. I decided education was the answer. When I have a university degree, I thought, then I will be intellectual enough to communicate well and connect with others. Then I will have a better job to earn a higher income, therefore improving my worth and the amount of time I can spend drinking in exotic places. The ongoing trail of positive feedback from professors for a job well done provided motivation and short-lived fulfillment for achieving small goals; another week, another assignment, and another grade that compared me to others. Debates, presentations, written reports, exams, I could get great results, and I felt somewhat accomplished. Outside of the valuable skillsets I acquired and the fancy pieces of paper that represented them, the one truly great thing to blossom from this experience is my ongoing friendship with Aliesha Huia.

From university assignment partners, day-drinking procrastinators, and Vietnam expats, we have often had many things in common. While our lives and paths are incredibly different, nevertheless they regularly intersect to this day, allowing us to reciprocate non-judgmental support for one another and to provide different perspectives of advice as we talk freely and decompress from the confusion of life. The benefit of having a close friend who is not directly "in the thick of it" with you has been an ongoing blessing and subject to many laughs as we share stories of the best times, the great moments, the questionable choices, and always have a door open for the other no matter where we are in the world—a friend in the truest meaning of the word.

Aliesha and I attended university in a rather isolated area. Before committing to my degree, I had never been to this area and it didn't take long to figure out that it would not be my long-term home or even a place I would have chosen as a short-term home if it wasn't for my desire to study. As those university years seemed to stretch on forever, I was finding less resonance with the nightclubs and spending more time with Aliesha, who liked to cook and bake, who had a herb garden and grew sunflowers, who was an avid reader, ran for fitness, and was the first person who got me thinking about my dietary choices and the products I used. She planted seeds of conscious awareness that I couldn't recognize at the time but have nourished me ever since. Just through being her beautiful self in this weird world and with the bonus of the kindness she has always offered me. We both left our university town as soon as possible after graduation, going our separate ways internationally with occasional meetups and regular virtual connections.

At the time, I felt compelled to see the world, having decided this would be the most desirable way to spend my time on earth. I always believed I could do anything I set my mind to, but every possible option felt limited to me. Everything that came to mind seemed excruciating, boring, didn't resonate, or was just plain meh. So, travel it was. I assumed I would find my place in the world somewhere else in the world.

The Healing Journey to Authenticity

Meaning in Experience

I hiked in the Himalayas, visited the Baltic Sea, wandered a thousand temples in Bagan, Myanmar, went bungee jumping in Queenstown, diving in Thailand, skydiving in Mexico, lived in a chateau in France, marveled at the beauty of the Amalfi Coast, met the limitations of Google Maps in Venice, and slept in the Sandhills of the southwestern Portuguese coast while hiking part of the Rota Vicentina. All the while, I involved myself in communities as a teacher, I volunteered, and I learned about cultures. I was well-travelled, well-experienced, and considered a professional. I met goals, I took a few photos, had a few beverages, witnessed others in their truth, and was invited by many locals into their lives. Travelling was exciting and more enjoyable than anything else I had experienced, but this consistent country-hopping masked my resistance to human connection. I lived out of a carry-on backpack and had no fixed abode, ties, or connections to anywhere or anything. I was impressed with myself. I was proud of the life I had made. But I did begin to wonder if I was maybe missing something. Maybe I could have been squeezing more out of these experiences, or maybe I should feel more for the life I was living.

I leaned further into teaching and further away from the bottom-line-orientated world of business. I witnessed children and their interactions, I observed them feel and express themselves openly, honestly, and often joyfully, always without shame. They were simply being. I provided education and tried to be a good example of an adult, and they offered their own lessons of innocence to me.

My European passport had made a considerable section of land easily accessible to me, but I craved something new and exciting. I scrolled Skyscanner using the search flights to 'everywhere' function to see if inspiration would draw me in. Bulgaria to Mexico City. This trip would be quite the adventure, I would travel through east-

Chapter 7

ern Europe, grazing the surface of a few countries: Austria, Czech Republic, Slovakia, Hungary, Romania, and Bulgaria, before departing from Sophia Airport to visit Hannah Bell Booth, a brilliant and inspiring person whose friendship led me on adventures that uncapped my awareness of my potential, I consider this relationship to be an all-round highlight of my travels to date.

The Hike to Not the Highest Lake in the World

Hannah and I had met in Mandalay, Myanmar both teaching at a school there. Our friendship blossomed and I was blessed with her companionship and instigation for exciting excursions. The most noteworthy venture began at breakfast in the hotel when she had initially convinced me to stay in Mandalay and complete a year contract with the school. A year seemed like an awfully long time to stay in one place, but she had some compelling reasoning, and I agreed to look into it. The next morning, however, I was greeted with the news that she had changed her mind. "I want to hike the Annapurna Circuit after our summer contract is up," Hannah informed me. "Do you want to come with me?" "Sure," I answered. I had never heard of the Annapurna Circuit. Hannah filled me in on a few details of her plan, and I was in. We met up in Nepal a few weeks later and found a bus to the trailhead.

The highly-regulated recreational activities from my Western upbringing did little to prepare me for what I was about to encounter. I had purchased my hiking permit, and in my mind, that was all that was required for this trek, so without a second thought, I was off into the Himalayan mountains with a pair of runners, a lightly packed backpack, and a blog article that Hannah had downloaded. The sole fell off my runners on the first full day of hiking, and it turns out that the blog article was published before a semi-recent earthquake, so the trail had changed significantly since then. Deterred not, our interest was piqued upon hearing rumours that the highest lake in the world was just a day trek off the main trail. Well, we're here, we decided we may as well go. I had my permit, right? What could go wrong?

The hike to the base camp of Tilicho Lake was when the "personal discernment penny" dropped for me. This penny has since been cashed in countless times as I deepen my intention to make deliberate choices for myself based on my truth and not what other people, established institutions, or spirits (for that matter) advise me to do. Hannah was ahead listening to Beyoncé in her earphones, I was snapping pics trying to capture the full drama of the mountains. We were walking along when suddenly the trail disappeared, and I was scrambling along the side of an almost vertical mountain slope, kilometres down, rocks falling from above. I was slipping and sliding downwards, caught in the gradual landslide, struggling on all fours in a blind panic to reach the safety of the trail on the other side. Terrifying. Where was Hannah? I ran to find her. She was just around the corner in shock, breathing, crying, processing. I sat down next to her as we recounted our experience. Yikes. Given this was a side trek off the main trail, we soon realized that we still had to hike back along that same death-defying section, but that was a problem for another day, so on we went.

The trek to Tilicho Lake is probably the hardest section of hiking and the most strenuous physical exertion I have experienced. I was not in shape, never had been. I was at one of my heaviest points in life after eating my way through Europe and Southeast Asia. I had decided to quit smoking recently but still drank rather heavily. I didn't even do a simple Google search before arriving in Nepal to hike. All this to say that I may have been slightly ill-prepared for the day ahead.

We were up at 5 a.m. with other base camp hikers looking to

Chapter 7

reach Tilicho Lake that day; I chucked a couple of essential items in my sleeping bag case to carry with me, a drink bottle, maybe a lip balm and a couple of cookies. We started the ascent in the snow, and a few metres in, I was exhausted and struggling to find evidence in my mind that I would be able to reach our destination. We made it up the first hard mountain in a blizzard. I couldn't see the person directly in front of me and just kept placing one foot ahead of the next. I tried to take a photo, but there was too much white, and I felt like I might fall off the mountain if I didn't focus. I had been hearing what I thought was thunder and could even feel the earth vibrating; the hikers ahead of us turned around to announce that they would head back down the mountain because of the AVALANCHES we were experiencing during this blizzard.

My thoughts consisted of: *This cannot be real. What am I doing here? How did this happen?*

Hannah and I followed them back down, concerned about what I now knew were avalanches and not thunder. Once we arrived back at base camp, the sun had come out, and the weather seemed to have cleared, so we turned around and started the hike again. I was already tired of dragging myself up the mountain. I was over it, but something kept pushing me forward. We hiked and hiked, up and up. The group dispersed, and we connected with some other slower hikers, which added a welcome dynamic to our duo as Hannah and I were getting a little cranky at each other. We completed the mountain part of the hike and could see miles of steep switchbacks ahead of us—I was not impressed. I was, in fact, quite miserable. Other hikers were returning down the mountain and advising us to just go back as the weather wasn't clear enough to even see the lake, and even after the switchbacks, there were several kilometres of deceptively difficult hiking through thick snow.

Options were discussed, I was quiet, firm-lipped, annoyed, tired, and hungry. It was my turn to share input, and I said I wanted to press on. I didn't, but logically, I'd come too far to only come this far. Determination that I didn't know I had was at work within. So we continued, for hours, barely able to breathe, through thick snow with burned faces and wobbly legs, surviving off the occasional Oreo cookie Hannah had wisely packed. We were struggling. Well…not all of us. One girl from the Czech Republic who had joined our group was easily strolling along and talking non-stop. I stayed several steps behind to avoid her conversation while Hannah was entertaining it for the most part, until she dropped a truth bomb that prompted both of us to stare her down. We were giving ourselves a pep talk and trying to find motivation in the feat of reaching the "highest lake in the world," when our new Czech friend chimed in, "This isn't the highest lake in the world, in fact..." "You're going to have to stop talking!" Hannah cut her off, not wanting to hear this under our current circumstances.

The hike seemed to go on forever, and there was no lake in sight—until there was. We made it to the edge of the peak, the clouds parted, the sun graced us, the weather calmed, and Mother Nature welcomed us to our destination. Our dedication had paid off. It was breathtaking, incredible, and to this day, one of the greatest accomplishments of my life.

After completing the Annapurna Circuit and a few days sleeping in Pokhara, Hannah and I went our separate ways—me to Poland and her for more travel within Nepal—before heading to Mexico City where we would reunite.

Mexico

Before accepting Hannah's invitation, Mexico had not been on my radar at all. I had lumped it in with North America and hadn't considered it a desirable travel destination. Until I arrived and dis-

Chapter 7

covered Mexico to be vast, diverse, culture rich, filled with kindness and beauty, and different from what I had experienced in my home country and my travels so far. It would take longer than my usual three months to experience Mexico.

This is the place where I started to really develop as myself, where I first began to feel energy and wonder if there was something more than just this physical life. I began meditating, setting boundaries, and started to understand the power of choice. I found that my perception is everything, and that I can change my perception, to create my life from the inside of my mind outwards.

I learned how to choose compassion for humanity and integrate a deeper love for fellow members of my species. This came through an understanding that everyone is doing the best they can with where they are at. Now this is not to insinuate that everyone is trying their best to be a good person or to consciously participate within the world in a positive way. This is to say that they are doing their best to exist under their current circumstances, traumas, belief systems, and values. For some this may look like lying or stealing to gain more resources or items of value to them—they are doing their best to grasp the opportunities that they see based on their current and subsequent thought processes. For others, this may look like intentional healing practices to release trauma and reconnect with their bodies after abuse or starting their own business to find financial freedom and help others. We ultimately are one, and when we heal one, we heal all. My mother put it well when she told me, "What goes around comes around." The impact of everything we do or be is part of our creative energy: every thought, word, and action is creative and at a certain frequency. Loving thoughts and actions vibrate higher than resentful thoughts or actions producing ripples of love in our environments. You are that which you create and you create that which you are. Connecting with these concepts heightened my commitment to purposeful decision-making in all areas of my life and I became increasingly more deliberate with my participation in the world around me.

I had committed to the idea that I lived in an abundant universe full of infinite possibilities and started to wonder, what else was possible? If I can have or do anything, what is that I ultimately desire? I was limited by my ability to think of something incredible enough to demand from the universe.

But sometimes whatever or whoever you need will simply present themselves. Through a string of seemingly random events, I eventually found myself volunteering at a botanical garden where I received the biggest sign of being on the right path: Neil Gerlowski (an incredible example of how to be a human being, a man whose zest for life, adventurous spirit, loving nature, and consistent companionship inspire me daily). Our connection swept me off my feet in an instant and has been the catalyst for so much personal growth. He provided the stability, grounding, and unconditional love that gave me a home and roots in the city of Puerto Vallarta. It is through having these earthly needs met that I have been able to allow myself the exploration into all that is, to derive new meanings in life, and to connect with spiritual realms and beings from or in other places—regardless of whether or not these aspects of my experience are true for him he remains an endless source of support.

Our decision to unite as a couple was perfect timing for the 2020 lockdowns. While the world was in chaos, I was in love and experiencing blessing after blessing in my new relationship. Armed with a machete, endless botanical knowledge, and a fascinating appreciation for the earth, Neil would lead us on hikes through the jungle to waterfalls and river headwaters. We'd explore hidden beaches and attend indigenous dance ceremonies to express gratitude for Madre Tierra.

Chapter 7

My Friend, the Messenger

I was experiencing life fully and was grounded in what was truly important to me. I grew more connected to my experience, and it was around this point that my intuition kicked into overdrive. My awareness of things I didn't understand or necessarily believe in, such as energies, angels, and spirits, started to become apparent.

What if what is true for us is obscenely different from anything we have heard about from others? What if the information I am perceiving and the method in which I am perceiving it is not acknowledged, widely accepted, or verifiable by Google? Am I going crazy?

Rosetta, my now dear friend, opened up a whole new meaning to the term "infinite possibilities" and exposed me to intricacies of divine truths that continue to change my perspectives and understanding of the human experience. She spoke of having traumas healed by angels, of spiritual interaction, of energetic awareness, quantum physics, our highest good, the importance of cleansing our mind, body, and soul, and explained that she was gifted the awareness and understanding of this information from God and ascended masters. I was there with her during the integration process, from a person living their life in a "normal" way to that of a divine messenger using her free will to share knowledge and integrate such knowledge into her own life. This woman who had once giggled at my meditation practice and was wide-eyed in shock when I told her I didn't consume animal, factory, or overly processed products now teaches others the pathway toward healthier consumption and participation with all areas of life.

At the time, her explanations of miracle healings, talking to angels, and being guided by divine beings to share messages were completely foreign concepts in my world and seemed unreal, but some part of me knew her words to be true, and I knew that I would be there to support her on this journey.

The Healing Journey to Authenticity

I had turned away from my studies and career in the business field but found new meaning with those skills when Rosetta hired me to help her increase her reach and impact with her work. She was my first client in the spiritual business niche and I was delighted at the realization that those years of experience were not wasted. There are plenty of people with aligned values who can benefit from my skills while I help them spread their magic and light to the world. Hallelujah.

I was also there as her confidant and friend and often one of the first people to receive new messages and awarenesses she had to share. This gift has fast-tracked my positive progression with choices pertaining to personal health and well-being in huge ways. Rosetta has also provided me with theoretical tools to transmute energy that no longer serves me and has allowed me to witness and experience her connections with beings from beyond this physical world which paved the way for an understanding of my own awareness and gifts in this area. An awareness of energies and beings that I had been unconsciously blocking out my entire life.

This newfound acuity ranged from terrifying to exciting, fun, and back to terrifying with a side of self-traumatizing. I received countless loving and valuable insights about myself and life that I cherish to this day. I was guided further into self-expression with writing poetry, creating for the sole purpose of creating, an increase in love for myself and for the miracle that is my body. I had spirits entertaining me, telling jokes, helping find items to buy and gifts to give, and also distracting me from my place on earth. At one point I was guided to have my puppy trained as a service dog for dissociative episodes; luckily, he was a fast learner because this was an invaluable aid. I would fall into deep trancelike states with channelling and would be gradually guided back to this world through touch and sound such as dog licks, barks, or gentle bites depending on how long he had been trying to get my attention. I spent a lot of time outside enjoying life, but simple human necessities like time, eating, connecting with people, and house cleaning would have been lost without Salty.

Initially I felt as though all my prayers were answered now that I had "secret friends" to discuss my plans and life with; however, just as personal discernment and boundaries are important with people, this is possibly even more true with non-physical beings. While some of the most positive influences I have connected with exist in this nonphysical state, so do some of the most sneaky and negative. At one point this experience led me to hope for insanity as an alternative to the constant exchange I was having with spirits, and ultimately resulted in an exorcism to help remove entities that decided they wanted to be in my body. My fear was rampant and the negative situation with entities had brought to light the deep-seeded areas in my psyche that needed healing. It provided the opportunity to get very personal with myself and pursue knowledge from energy workers, teachers, shamans, spiritualists, and healers of all descriptions who have helped me to further understand the unseen forces of this universe. No longer limited in my ability to see the possibilities, another door opened for me to be in service to people awakening to their own awareness as a counsellor.

Peace in My Present

Now while I travel, I have the comfort of Mexican residency and a current address in a city I call home, friends to visit internationally, I have my husband by my side, as well as Salty, our dog, while we hike the Peruvian mountains and participate in the beautiful community of Písac in the Sacred Valley.

Life is no longer happening to me; I am creating it with every thought, desire, and consideration. I have learned that the healing and self-discovery journey is beautifully never-ending and that focusing my attention outside of *my* present is not the answer. I take deliberate moments to enjoy the experience of being me, having a body, of feeling connected, of experiencing love, of exchanging energy with the earth. She who never judged me, she who homes me, who took care of me in all scenarios, I love to spend time with you Pachamama.

What is true for me, may not be true for you, and what is true for me in this moment may not be true for me in the next moment as I learn, become, unlearn, uncover, and reveal new layers of awareness, knowledge, and understanding. My journey of conscious authenticity has been an advancement of personal truth and self-trust. To shed the mindset that somebody else knows better and allow my intuitive knowing to be the truth that I need to reach my goals, to trust in myself and my experience, and to allow others to be where they are regardless of what this means for their interaction with me. Nothing is personal. Every person's behaviour and treatment of others is merely a reflection of where they are within themselves.

When we master the quality of self-trust—the ability to recognize and commit to what is true for us—then we are no longer at the mercy of other influences. We can trust ourselves to make decisions in alignment with that truth, committing to showing up for ourselves in the most authentic way and offering ourselves the freedom of being us without the limitations or stipulations from all that exists outside of who we truly are.

Chapter 7

About Sky Gerlowsi

Hailing from New Zealand with Irish and Māori ancestry, Sky Gerlowski initially attended Australian and New Zealand universities to study justice, business, marketing, and education. With interests in energetic modalities, languages, and the universe at large, she continues to learn and develop her skill sets including the recent completion of a counselling qualification.

Sky's lifelong commitment to personal development makes her an advocate for the universal pursuit of collective healing through personal growth to improve humanity as a whole. Grounded in the principle of interconnectedness, she champions mindful community engagement and fosters awareness of the limitless potential of individual choice and actions.

Her passion for nurturing a conscious world is evident in her diverse pursuits as an esteemed children's educator, a spiritual business strategist, and a counsellor. Sky's work is enriched by her ongoing travels, faith, and spiritual perspective. She channels her boundless energy into facilitating the purposeful endeavours of those spreading light and brightening the future of our world.

linktr.ee/skygerlowski

8

Consciously Rewriting My Story: The Journey from Victim to Creator

By Angela Wieland

*I am not what happened to me,
I am what I choose to become.*

— Carl Jung

Consciously Rewriting My Story: The Journey from Victim to Creator

By Angela Wieland

I have reached a point in my life where I am all about radical authenticity. I hadn't known this eluded me until fairly recently as I have always thought of myself as an independent thinker and more of a leader than a follower. Yet I hadn't realized the scope to which my past and external influences, tempered through my unique internal filter, had separated me from my true self. To me, being authentic speaks to being unapologetically who I am, of completely allowing, becoming, and owning who I was born to be, of living in alignment. It's about being guided by what truly sparks enthusiasm within, embodying my unique skills, gifts, and urges, and contributing what I am here to be, do, and share by being unmistakably me. But, perhaps paradoxically, therein lies the dilemma. Authenticity requires that we know who we are. It's impossible to be true to ourselves if we are disconnected from our essence, concealed beneath conditioning, fear, and ego. Since becoming more consciously aware, I've been observing myself and have witnessed how my thoughts and subsequent emotions vary so considerably and can radically shift my whole perspective and identity even—often without anything changing externally. It is all happening within me. I mean, of course, there are occurrences here and there that bring about sorrow or joy, but the way we define what our emotions and responses mean, the filter we choose to see them through, makes all the difference in our experience of life.

For example, as I considered what to write, where to start or what my actual message is, I felt resistance, doubt, and potential judgment. What might I possibly share that could have meaning and/or relevance for others? While I am aware that my willingness to be vulnerable is a strength, I nonetheless can feel hesitant, shy away from expressing my truth and claiming my personal power, and minimize any contribution I might make. This ingrained practice stems from allowing my self-doubt and fear to historically run the show. Without awareness, I tend to perpetuate more of the same. Now, I aim to be mindful that I am creating my reality moment by moment, so it is imperative I monitor my perspective which, until now, has been linked in large part to past experiences.

For the longest time I had no idea that I was identifying with these often-self-defeating thoughts. I believed they were who I was which led to so much (in fact a lifetime of) despair. In one minute I would feel devastated by the finality of a breakup and the loss of both what was and what could have been. In the next, a wave of freedom and sovereignty would wash over me, having been inspired and motivated to finally take action. In moments like these, I would feel deeply, reminded of my connection to source, to God, and shift to a place of resolution and trust. I could rise above the loss in order to continue forward, undistracted and detached, dedicated to my own journey of healing, expression, and movement toward purpose. Then, once again, I would be touched by a memory and triggered into deep sobbing. Such is the nature of life.

It is in our momentary acceptance or resistance, determined by our position and our patterning, that determines the course of our life and our subsequent suffering or joy. The more we can align our choices with our essence, the more things will flow for us, and the more magical life can be. It comes down to faith and trust in ourselves, in life, and in God; a belief that everything serves a purpose and works out for our highest good. As cliché as it may sound, all is happening for us. The universe is conspiring in our favour even if it seems otherwise.

I had been actively looking for my purpose forever and a day, failing to realize that disconnection from myself was at the core of the issue. How could I possibly know what I am meant to be doing or how I am to serve if I am not clear on, or aware of, who I truly am? Though I have provided hypnotherapy and various types of coaching for years, this internal breakthrough has reignited my desire to be of service to others, specifically in finding, reclaiming, and honouring the parts within me that may have been masked, lost, or abandoned over the years. The greatest gift we can give the world is to uniquely shine our light and express our vision.

In the Beginning: The Seeds of Inauthenticity and Losing Myself

I was a dreamy child who spent many days lying in the grass staring up at the shapes of the clouds. Like many of us growing up in a dysfunctional home and being a highly sensitive individual, I felt extremely unsafe and trapped. This fear manifested itself in a few ways. For one, my mind and body began to develop mechanisms to create a sense of security. My active imagination, above average intelligence, and "high strung" nervous system did their best. Inevitably, though, it created an inner situation which ultimately superseded the external environment I was trying to manage becoming a source of torment, suffering, and imprisonment.

I first met with a psychologist around the age of ten or twelve, I don't really recall. A lot of details were blocked out. When I was about fifteen, I was diagnosed with obsessive compulsive disorder (OCD), generalized anxiety, depression, and post-traumatic stress disorder (PTSD) and I had previously struggled with major sleep disturbances. I started to act out and began hanging out with kids from the "other side of the tracks"—a rather unsavoury social circle—and started drinking, doing drugs, and later developed an eating disorder. By twenty-two, I was taking the maximum permissible dose of an antidepressant, along with an anti-anxiety medication and something else to help me sleep. I used to joke that I was like Elvis in his later years.

There were also physical issues. I missed nearly half my sophomore year of high school. While there was for sure some straight-up delinquency as all my friends were drop-outs and I hated school, a greater contributing factor was being legitimately sick with chronic strep throat, bronchitis, and sinusitis (all of which I believe were physical manifestations of the deep yet buried grief and shame I felt). At least one of my instructors was hesitant to award me with the "A" grade my work had earned due to my excessive absence. These absences, along with tardiness, would continue into my work life and career earning me many reprimands and eventual terminations.

But beyond the mental, emotional, and physical ailments that have plagued me, one of the deepest sources of discontent was the disconnection from my soul, my true essence that developed as a result of the way I internalized my earlier circumstances. I convinced myself to become who I thought I should be. This charade has stalked me my whole life. Accompanying me for years was deep insecurity, low self-worth, and a lack of belief in my capabilities, all the usual suspects one might expect to see in association with deep trauma, leading me to play it safe and to remain small.

However, this lack of authenticity, of pursuing things which did not truly interest or excite me as a true passion would, was another ultimately devastating and "time wasting" component (but also, as I see it now, a necessary part of the process). But, as with pretty much everything in life, nothing exists in isolation. All is interwoven in a complex tapestry, one thing feeding into the next, which is how patterns and cycles develop. These patterns then feed into our perception of identity and perpetuate, in this case, a disassociation from self. For me, this resulted in shoving myself into situations and jobs I was capable of but were not the most optimal fit.

Choosing Safety over Authenticity

Although I have always been a creative person, I chose to rely on and found safety and security within the constraints and structure provided by my analytical brain. I had an affinity for art and fashion and was told by some that I was talented. Yet, I did not feel my creative abilities were adequate due to an overwhelming need to be in control and perfect when the rest of my world was so unstable and unsafe. Instead, I decided to pursue what was more measurable and objective. Though it did not particularly light me up inside, I was good at math and I liked it well enough. I represented our high school at the math and science fair/conference, being encouraged by all my instructors, but most importantly, it gave me a sense of security, and looked "good on paper" as opposed to the subjective nature of art, writing, etc. The answer to a math problem is either right or wrong, and this felt safe at the time.

I was already judging myself critically and harshly. My father had no tolerance for "stupidity," so it was not acceptable to be a child, nor human, and though I was a top performer, always being in the TAG (Talented and Gifted) and later AP (Advanced Placement) programs in middle, junior and high school, any time there was less than perfection, I would hear about it. Added to that, my father impressed upon me the belief that it was only a matter of time before one's passions, if pursued professionally, would be reduced to a mere "job."

I clearly remember around the age of fifteen or sixteen having a bit of an existential meltdown over the notion that work is pretty much a necessary evil, basically a living hell. My mother was clearly not into her job and was more or less demonstrably suffering through each day. I despised school; the thought that I would be shackled for the rest of my life to some nine-to-five employment situation once school was over was almost too much to bear. Of course, now I know there exists a multitude of options, but at that moment, I could only see the choices I considered possible according to my programming and limited knowledge base.

So while I started out pursuing psychology and photography in college, two subjects for which I was a natural fit, I eventually talked myself out of both through my lack of belief in my own creativity, coupled with my parents' influence, as well as societal conditioning. If my inspiration would eventually turn into indifference or even disdain, I might as well go after the most lucrative option. Even though I was a top student encouraged by my psychology professor, with a clear affinity for the subject, I overrode it all due to my limited views of myself. Additionally, my nineteen-year-old self wondered what I would do with a psychology degree since I was a bit of a loner, and didn't really like a lot of people. I also thought of my own psychiatrist, who always struck me as a little crazy, and felt I did not want to encourage any more neurosis than I already deemed present within me. I remember being quite angry and angsty at this time in my life due to existing family dynamics, as well as past abuse. This was reflected in my unconventional and "out there" attire and attitude, deeply rooted in punk rock culture, which espoused an "on the edge of society vibe" for which I had proudly and unabashedly taken a lot of slack, especially during my early to mid-teenage years. In those areas of my life, I was oozing confidence and pride despite the adverse reactions I received from others. I relished being contrarian and marching to my own drum. It gave me a sense of power and showcased my innovative and natural leadership.

Nevertheless, I fell back on my aptitude for math and decided to switch to finance thinking I'd make the big bucks in investment banking, stock trading, or financial analysis. Thus continued my abandonment of self in pursuing something because of X, Y, Z instead of the genuine excitement or joy it would bring me. After receiving coveted scholarships and internships, I graduated with honours and while I possessed the ability to do this type of work, it was most definitely not the best for me. While I was provided many incredible opportunities, I could never quite get it together to truly be successful, or to take myself seriously. I was able to interview well and land amazing jobs, and in some cases perform quite well to a certain extent being seen as a "golden child" initially. But typically it wouldn't take long for me to become rather overwhelmed, stressed, and operate out of a sense of being in over my head. I would start to implode, self-sabotage, or just underperform. Though I was strong out of the gate, I often felt incompetent, like I was posturing, pretending to be someone I was not.

Retrospectively, I realized I was never fully invested in the majority of the jobs I had. I lacked interest and engagement which ultimately led to indifference to the outcome. My primary motivation was fueled by the desire to make money, couched in a continuing plague of deep-seated insecurity and feeling inadequate that permeated all areas of my life.

A Wake-up Call

I have had a habit of forcing myself to do things which often accompanied the belief I needed to push myself to grow to get used to or over something, and if I didn't, I was allowing my fear to get the better of me. But in looking back, I was often overriding what my intuition or internal compass was directing me toward or steering me from. A lot of this comes from not knowing the true me and instead relying on the stories I created from what I learned through conditioning from my family and society, as well as my experienced trauma. My trust in self had always been lacking.

Historically, my relationships also reflected my instability, insecurity, and lack of connection with reality. I was projecting my traumas onto those around me and constantly living in fear. My mind had full control, and I was never able to be present. I was either reliving something traumatizing from the past, or filled with apprehension about what might happen next. My thoughts perpetuated the suffering well after the actual external circumstances had passed. Such is the effect of trauma. I had effectively put myself in a prison where I remained for decades of my life.

This last year, 2023, was a pivotal one. After pursuing yet another vocation for which I possessed the skill set but was just going through the motions, and despite much promise, it delivered nothing in the end. Although I was tempted to take that personally, to use it against myself to feel bad and to continue pushing, I instead took stock, and honestly admitted I lacked passion, subsequent investment, and was merely doing it in an attempt to make money. I had lost touch with who I truly am and the gifts that I am best meant to use in service to

Chapter 8

the world. I decided to take a step back into the abyss of "what now." After years of feeling stagnant and desperate to find my calling, it gradually became clear that I had been trying to put the cart before the horse. This realization came in tandem with another failed relationship wherein the same childhood fears were projected. I didn't know how, but I knew something had to shift. It was not a lightbulb moment, as I had been struggling for years, but as they say, when the student is ready, the teacher will appear, and so it was.

I was casually checking a social media account when an ad caught my eye. It was a workshop on transformation and awakening, in part achieved through detachment from our thoughts. I saw it at least three times before it incited any kind of call to action within me. It was by donation and I contributed very little, having limited faith and low expectations. But something inside me nudged me forward and I made a decision to sign up which, as simple as that might sound, was meaningful in and of itself; decisions often did not come easily for me due to overthinking and a lack of trust in myself.

I certainly did not expect what I experienced—I was one of the handful chosen to participate out of a couple thousand on the live Zoom call. That in itself was a significant sign to me despite the fact I felt I presented on camera as a bit of a chaotic mess. As I was explaining where and how I felt stuck and frustrated, it so happened that was the moment some guys showed up to deliver my washing machine. In an effort to not lose this perceived once-in-a-lifetime opportunity, I juggled both on camera: directing the four men in my home while simultaneously closing my eyes and attempting to reflect on the questions that were being posed to me. In truth it actually couldn't have been more perfectly representative, reflecting my tendency to take on too much combined with a feeling I would otherwise miss out, which typically results in overwhelm. But, on that call, I felt what I had not truly felt in a very long time … hope.

The Healing Journey to Authenticity

I was told I am not my story.

In that moment, it was as though an impossibly loud bell had sounded and the message was as clear as day and registered as never before; I realized how deeply identified I was with my point of view, which often saw me as a victim, and how faithfully attached I was to my story. This rude truth smacked me upside the head: I was keeping myself stuck via what I had created and accepted about who I was. I also became aware that my nervous system was overactive and contributing to the repetitive toxic patterns. Additionally and miraculously, during one of the later meditations, I was able to let go and felt the energy within me activate in a way it never had previously.

As someone who has been habitually stuck in my head and super disconnected from my body, I was kind of beside myself. I was finally starting to see movement, literally and figuratively, as the energy trapped within my body was allowed to express itself. I was able to momentarily release the control of my mind, which genuinely amazed me. I felt so grateful and connected to the Divine which had clearly conspired to lead me to this teacher. It was up to me to heed the call. Though I did not have the finances for the intensive course that was the next step, and indecision was my standard go-to response, I felt compelled to take action and I enrolled. I saw the possibility, though blurry, of an alternate reality, a potential way out of the seemingly never-ending cycle. I became aware of the fact that I had the power to choose differently, and that it was up to me to change my identity and mindset from victim to creator. So I began the process of deconditioning my mind, reprogramming my outlook, and consciously rewriting my story…

I had to first and foremost accept responsibility that this is an inside job. I also had to realize that after decades of running this as my operating system, it was going to take diligent work on my behalf to loosen the grip, to essentially detox my mind, but also my nervous system and body, to no longer be defined by the past. What took fifty years to develop was going to take some conscious and steadfast effort to dismantle. I became aware of my language, of how I was speaking to myself, about myself and the world at large in powerfully invalidating ways. Words are spells; we create what we broadcast as our "truth." We attract and become what we announce to ourselves and the universe.

I had also accepted circumstances I did not like as beyond my control from the mindset that things were happening to me. I had to realize that I was attracting and creating my reality based on my thoughts and beliefs, and relating to the lessons I still needed to learn. As motivational speaker Les Brown has said, "You don't get what you want in life, you get who you are!"

We get what we tolerate—from ourselves, from others, and from life in general. Once I came to terms with that, I realized that I am the only one who can create a different reality for myself. That was both empowering and scary. It was a bit of a wake-up call. No one or thing was going to save me. This is an inside job. In my belief system, the spiritual realms are there to support us if we only ask. So I began an active relationship of talking and working with God, my guides, and angels to help me. Faith and connection to a higher power has been a crucial key for me.

The Road to Authenticity

As a historically chronic overthinker who was thick as thieves with my mind, it was absolutely essential in my evolution that I separate myself from the incessant, unhelpful chatter, and if required, consciously choose to change the channel, i.e. think of something else. In tandem, I reminded myself that my ego was likely going to fight like hell to maintain the status quo that had until now been my life directive and path. I started to catch the thoughts, to see them with detachment (not always, but that is the goal), and to accept that my ego is necessary, but sometimes not my friend. Prioritizing my daily meditation practice became a useful tool to allow me to witness my thoughts, feelings, and judgments, and see them for what they are.

Another component was reconnecting to my intuition. I have been told repeatedly by an assortment of friends, family, and therapists that my intuition is one of my greatest gifts, but I was always surprised to hear this as would be expected from someone under the spell of an overly rational mind. I saw in several instances how I had overridden my intuitive hunches and nudges which, when ignored, generally ended up circling me back to another version of the same unlearned lesson. As I deepened my connection with my inner knowing, reflected back to me by my body and emotions, and learned to trust the messages I felt, or rather deeply knew, there was no thinking necessary. Thinking was often what got me into trouble. It was what led me to disconnect from and abandon my true self, to rely too heavily on my left brain, and to need to analyze absolutely everything from every angle. It kept me separate from my real desires and often paralyzed with confusion and subsequent drifting due to an inability to make a decision. Or conversely, resulted in a decision made from the rational mind but completely devoid and divorced from both my heart and my gut.

This led me to confront the part of myself that needed attention: my body. As someone who lived chronically in my head and had spent much of life dissociated due to my defence mechanisms, I was quite disembodied. My nervous system was often overstimulated and in need of grounding as a result of the trauma and painful associations that had formed my reality. Breathwork and other somatic practices have been helpful to reconnect with my body. Simple walks on the beach barefoot, or even just allowing the tears to come when felt, can be profound. I am learning to let my guard down and let myself be supported and seen. I realize now, though I was going through the motions before, seeing therapists, going to ayahuasca ceremonies, and desperately wanting to breakthrough, I simply wasn't ready. I was trying instead of allowing. I was still in so much fear, I couldn't let go of my need to control. It still can be hard, but I am learning to surrender.

I also came to understand that my frustration of having my purpose elude me up until this point was very understandable. The frustration reinforced my perceived need to somewhat randomly select this or that to plug myself into as a means to make income. I soon realized that trying to find my purpose in the state I had been chronically living was next to impossible. I was getting ahead of myself. It was time to rediscover myself, to circle back to who I really am, and so began what has turned into an almost monomaniacal pursuit of authenticity.

It started with a gradual, but then adamant, disconnection from that which I had pursued out of ability as opposed to passion. At that point, whenever others asked me, or I asked myself, what I would do if there were no obstacles, I truly had no answer. That was how disconnected I was from my being. I had been so caught up in the doing, in the pushing, out of avoidance, habit, nervous system wiring, and an unrelenting inner directive, that I hadn't stopped to consider, to reflect, or to listen. In my mind, there had been no time for that. But answers (as with the best love relationships) often find us when we give up the chase and, instead, embrace life and what makes us enjoy living it.

I decided to substitute the non-stop self-flagellation that had been standard procedure for years with re-engaging in things that brought me joy. I signed up for an art class, did some travelling, and allowed myself time to read. I also had an epiphany: I had to make time (which I still find paradoxical) to slow down and allow myself to get out of doing, in order to sink into acceptance and being. It has been in these moments of quiet reflection and stillness that the messages—the whispers from spirit and my inner knowing—have begun to come.

Sharing the Perspective of Authenticity

One of the lessons I learned during the course last year is the importance of closing open tabs, of completing cycles, of freeing up space to make room for the new. To that end, I was recently deleting some files on my computer and ran across an old recorded session with a client (and myself as the practitioner). For some reason I felt compelled to listen. The main message I was relaying to him, which I urged repeatedly, was the importance of taking action, some sort of step forward, no matter how small, even though the road ahead may still be unclear. Ironically, I have also felt at times almost paralyzed, afraid to waste any more time or to make the wrong decision. Yet, it illustrates the magic and connection I feel and have felt with the Divine in being led and delivered to whatever is needed to propel me forward. How poignant that it was my own voice and advice. It was of course not lost on me, and I smiled, feeling such gratitude for my process. Through surrender, I am being led back to myself.

I am still very much a work in progress. Recently during an intuitive reading, I mentioned that it may be time for me to step up. I have had the feeling of drifting at sea for so long that at times I feel the need to take bold and decisive action as I had encouraged my client to do. This oracle coach responded, "Is it, or is it best to continue to be until your inner knowing prompts you?" She went on to say that rather than feeling as though I've been stagnating, why not see it as perfectly aligned with a grander vision that is allowing me the time and space for healing, evolution, and in turn for authenticity to re-emerge. It's yet another reminder that all is a matter of perspective, and to consider that, no matter the pain, frustration, or disappointment, things are happening for me, not to me. Each interaction, regardless of whether as a therapist, client, friend, partner, parent, or child, serves as a mutual exchange and an opportunity for reflection, growth, and self-realization.

I now understand what I had viewed as wasting either talent, time, effort, or all three, was ultimately just part of my path. It is only when I compare myself to others, their expectations, or the definitions of success constructed by society that I feel suffering, lack, or inadequacy. But the truth is we are all different and each of us on our own journey. Again, it comes down to perception. Some, who I may deem to have it all (especially when coming from the mindset I have been dismantling), may actually marvel at the freedom I have in my life and wish for the same sense of adventure for themselves.

I am coming to discover that all I have been through has not been for naught. I can see that my wounding, the road I travelled, the way I process things, and my sensitivities have all been perfect and divinely orchestrated to deliver me such a beautiful and amazing gift. I was meant to experience all that I have so I can shine a light to help others also remember, embrace, and embody their authenticity. I had to go through all that I did in order to understand all that I do—to be able to step into my purpose, my divine mission, and my creative genius. I'm still not sure exactly what that will look like, as it is still organically unfolding; it may always be a bit of a moving target. But I do trust that I am just where I need to be, and despite having nothing tangible to hold onto, I feel a sense of excitement of what is to come while simultaneously doing my best to live and be present in each moment along the way.

It is up to me, and to each of us, to consciously determine the lens through which we view the world and to focus on what we want as opposed to what we don't or what is missing. As one of my mentors says, we can't wait for the mirror to smile. It is our responsibility and within our power to become the creators of our lives. I have waited long enough. It's time to reclaim and embody my brilliance, to allow my true self to radiate. And so, reminding myself as often as is necessary, I smile.

Chapter 8

About Angela Wieland

Since childhood, Angela Wieland has been drawn to the mysteries of existence, exploring esotericism, metaphysics, psychology, altered states of consciousness, and spirituality. As a transformational hypnotherapist, empowerment coach, spiritual guide, astrologer, and toe reader, she channels her lifelong learning, experience, and empathy to help others reframe and transcend life's challenges. Her passion is in expanding consciousness, guiding clients to reconnect with their innate strength, wisdom, and sovereign personal power, transforming limitations into opportunities for expression, contribution, and purpose.

Angela's unique expertise has been sought internationally by the prestigious Four Seasons and St Regis luxury resorts in Punta de Mita, Mexico, as well as online. Her distinctive toe reading has been featured in publications such as Allure magazine and Well and Good.

Angela studied Mind Body Wellness at Southwest Institute of Healing Arts and holds a BS in Business/Finance from Portland State University. She appreciates the arts, design, travel, alternative medicine, and the natural world.

www.angela-wieland.com
angela.wieland@gmail.com

9

Transforming Grief Through Love —A Mother's Journey

By Tonda Eger-Chin

*Generally, by the time you are Real,
most of your hair has been loved off,
and your eyes drop out and you get loose in the
joints and very shabby.
But these things don't matter at all,
because once you are Real you can't be ugly,
except to people who don't understand.*

— **Margery Williams,** *The Velveteen Rabbit*

Transforming Grief Through Love —A Mother's Journey

By Tonda Eger-Chin

The Velveteen Rabbit started out as a "very splendid" little, stuffed toy rabbit whose heart was wounded in the process of loving and being loved by a small boy. Becoming tattered and worn over time, he "found himself in a trash heap" one day only to learn that being "Real isn't how you are made," it's a "thing that happens to you over time" when you face the heartbreak of loss or adversity. Your rough edges get rubbed off as you become more Real. In the end, the pain of life and loss brought the Rabbit to a state of being more alive.

Just like the rabbit lost the little boy he loved, so did I. But, more importantly, grief changed us both—our stuffing got replaced and our sawdust hearts eventually grew bigger and more alive. There are multitudes of daunting challenges we can face in life. With many

The Healing Journey to Authenticity

people struggling and feeling alone in their troubles, it's heartening to see how people can be so brave and strong in the face of life's storms and the deepest of losses. It is all part of their journey, their humanity, their time alive on the earth. Good things can grow out of hardship, like minerals melted into beautiful gemstones or coal crushed into a diamond. For me, I found that love is never lost. It stays within us, becoming magnified and limitless in the times we need it the most; there is always more of it to give.

As a clinical counsellor, I work with those who are suffering losses and great distress in different ways, and I see how suffering can be transformative, changing us into more of what we are meant to be. Revealing the essence of our true self and our Divine spiritual nature. I too have been in sad and painful places, and anyone who has lost a child can tell you the abyss of grief is deep and dark. It helps me care for my clients more because I see them in me and me in them. They, like me, are on the path of becoming more "real" like the Velveteen Rabbit. The Rabbit's story reminds me that the flaws, scars, and brilliant gifts that all come from life's lessons can go together. While time in darkness and despair is part of my story, it doesn't define me. It inspires who I want to be, who I can be, and how I can live up to that potential.

While there is the poignant pain in telling my story, there is healing in it, too. Perhaps it will inspire others to share their stories. When my clients are bravely and honestly owning and accepting their unique story, who they are and who they can be, I have more courage to embrace my own uniqueness in the world. And while our paths are not alike, we are all stumbling sometimes, feeling worn out and needing each other. I am lucky to get to see the Real in people and be part of their sacred and spiritual journey. They too are missing their button eyes and some of their fur has been "loved off." Just as the wondrous little rabbit was becoming more genuine, more

Chapter 9

authentically real, we too are in that process, and we can all lend a little of our light and love to those who are without it.

Remembering Evan

Even after twenty-five years I am still processing the loss of my baby boy. I feel the trauma in my body as I try to write this: my throat closes, my voice cracks. I feel a rush of tears. I can't get a breath as the memory of that pain surfaces. It has been so hard to utter the words "my son died; I lost my son." The grief that exists in me after so long can still be suffocating.

After a trip to the hospital to end the second miscarriage instead of waiting indefinitely for it to pass on its own, I felt as though my body was betraying me and wondered if I will ever have children to know and love. Then we tried the hard, stressful, expensive journey of infertility treatment. I heard the woman next to me say she was still trying after many years, and I felt the panic inside. Miraculously, it worked the first time and a blessing had been bestowed. Two babies after two soul-crushing miscarriages seemed magical! They were identical twins. They would complete each other. They were to be born on Christmas Day and that would make it all the more special.

But, as suddenly as it was good, it was very bad. At eleven weeks, we were told that one of our babies had anencephaly, a congenital birth defect that was "not compatible with life." And our two beautiful boys who would be mirrors of each other were now "dangerously" sharing a placenta that could, at any time, take them both. Spontaneous perinatal death. With that, stark options were offered. Abort them both as the chance of survival of the healthy baby is low. Inject the one baby's heart with a drug that would stop it and hope it would not stop the other's heart, too. Or continue forward, week by week, with a very unlikely good outcome. It was too much. It was too painful. How could we decide the fates of these two precious gifts?

The Healing Journey to Authenticity

My husband and I were in the crosshairs. What would we tell others week after week when they asked about our babies? We had been walking on air only to be plummeted into darkness. The expectation of joy had been erased. The only thing more unimaginable was if they both slipped away together, and I would deliver two babies who had died. It was possible that this complicated pregnancy would end with a cavernous emptiness where our family might have been. The doctor had looked at us that day and, shockingly, said, "If it wasn't for bad luck, you'd have no luck at all." His words cut like a dagger. The colour began fading out of our world. I remember my strong, optimistic husband pull the cross from his neck feeling God had betrayed us.

At that moment, I heard a strong audible voice in me that said, "Do not let your brother stumble:" a command in the Bible. My husband, my best friend, was stumbling, too. In a time when I felt no strength, God was calling me to hold tight, even though it seemed he had turned from us. I knew He was asking me to put aside my own fears while my husband struggled with hope and faith. I said "yes" to His request of me to stay steady and to keep moving ahead. Out of His great compassion that day, God was not silent and, in the end, we turned it all over to God whose ways are greater than ours.

So it began, week after week of carrying Baby A, Ryan, and Baby B, Evan, knowing at any moment we might lose them both. Time suspended. Ultrasounds, amniocentesis, scans where we would see them together in my belly. A brutal reminder that Evan was not okay and Ryan's life was at the mercy of fate. I was put on bedrest in the hospital for six weeks due to the great risk of pre-term labour from litres and litres of extra amniotic fluid that would have to be drained off with a needle in my belly. This triggered labour multiple times, and I was given painful medication to try to stop it, knowing each time could be the last. There was a risk of twin-to-twin transfusion

Chapter 9

where the placenta would be compromised, and Ryan could suffer from cerebral palsy, heart damage, and death. There would be no miracle, only a terrible roller coaster ride of worry and fear.

At night, anxiety would take over. There was no relief from the pressure of the extra litres of amniotic fluid and two babies in my small body. I slept sitting up at night so my heart wouldn't race. I was just coping one slow day at a time and making plans for a baby's burial from my hospital bed, not knowing if we would bury one boy or two. How could this happen when we so desperately wanted and loved these two boys? It was the love that carried us through.

It was November, cold and rainy. We had made it through thirty-six agonizing weeks. And then, suddenly, it was time. Ryan came first. One boy was here! His eyes met mine and his tiny hand grabbed the sheet as he was whisked away. There was still another to deliver. But this one I held for one hour and nineteen minutes while his heart slowly stopped beating. It was a moment when my husband and I stood between Heaven and Earth with our son, talking to him, telling him how much we would miss him, and that he would be loved forever.

He had moved in my belly, but now that he was here, he wasn't going to live. For months I had worried that each day might be his last. That I would wake up one morning to find that he had slipped away in the night while I was sleeping. What would that moment be like when I delivered him, and my husband and I would see his beautiful face but never take him home? And now it was here. I still wonder who he would have been. How would his presence have changed the lives of others? What would it have been like to not lose him, and to also not lose a part of me that could have been doing more and being more? What if my husband and I had not experienced the devastating level of stress the loss would bring? We would not watch him grow up and see ourselves in him. We had

163

assumed these things to be the natural progression of life, we had expected them. Instead, we were moved into a special category of parents whose child had died.

We took Evan to say goodbye to his brother. Placing the two of them together, Ryan put his arm tenderly around his brother's body. And then, they took him. We had to let him go. That is when the grief took root and settled in me for the last twenty-five years. But, at the same time, joy set in because Ryan stayed with us that day. It was a profound "bittersweetness" of having gained so much and lost so much. When we finally left the hospital with Ryan, our hearts happy and heavy, there in the sky was the most brilliant and breathtaking double rainbow in recognition of the two.

And then, we embarked on the next leg of the journey.

Magnifying Love

In the days following the birth, I remember being alone in my hospital room watching happy mothers visit their daughters with bouquets of flowers and teddy bears. Day after day, they would pass by my door with their smiles and excited voices, hugging their daughters who had just birthed them a grandchild. But my mother was gone. She died of cancer years before, but alcohol had stolen her life from me and my siblings well before that. I longed to be one of those daughters who could have the comfort of my mother. Out of this hurt came a fierce fire of love inside of me—a love magnified—that gave me strength to fight for my children when times were challenging.

The cost of losing a child was a devastatingly stressful journey that had been hard on us. I struggled with guilt that I couldn't save Evan, that I had failed him, and that I couldn't give him the life he should have had. But Ryan was here and needing us! We had to pour love and joy into our new baby even though we still felt the sagging weight of sadness all the time. The physical trauma of the pregnancy, the level of stress, and the loss had taken so much out of me physically and emotionally that I couldn't speak at my son's funeral. I should have spoken. I wanted to speak. People came to be with us but part of me was split in half, mute. The day was cold and windy with icy rain. There was a little white casket. I remember the baby's breath wreath slowly falling to the ground and my husband's father picking it up and putting it back on top of the casket, a small gesture of kindness to show that Evan was important. My father cried that day for the grandson he would never know. My husband, who is so strong and able to withstand hard things, spoke for us both, and I am forever grateful for that. It was important that we speak our son's name. Whenever someone said his name, it touched me deeply to hear it.

Miracles have happened since then. Some of the rips in our seams have been mended and smoothed by having two more children. "One in Heaven and three on Earth" is how I sometimes answer those who ask how many children I have. That question still stirs pain in me. I remind myself that I am not denying Evan if I do not mention the one in Heaven when it would change the conversation in a way that is not helpful. He is not lost because he is a part of me. There are those around me who still so generously and lovingly remember and honour the birth and death of Evan. I find that so healing and restoring to my heart.

My husband and I are so thankful to have had another son, Chase, a special light in this world. He is a loving, kind, and thoughtful person who tells me he loves me each time he comes into the house. Sometimes we look at each other and just start to giggle without knowing why. Maybe we see the playful part in each other. After Chase, we had a beautiful daughter, Morgan, who walks this earth as an "otherworldly" magical creature. I greatly admire her for her strength and commitment to challenging herself and others to be more authentic, to be true to themselves. She is a powerful teacher. Her graceful beauty often takes my breath away.

And, Ryan, the one we got to keep, is a miracle that defied all odds. He is funny, and wise and such a loving spirit. I am truly humbled by his ability to encourage and accept others so graciously. He is a transformer of people wherever he goes. We grieve for how life might have been different for him if he could have had this other part of him, his twin. If he did not have guilt wondering why he lived and Evan did not. We grieve what might have been with every milestone. But Ryan, being a great gift, brings us so much joy.

My husband, who is strong, wise, and brave, reminds me to take time to remember Evan. As a family, the five of us will go to the cemetery to stand by the small headstone as a chance to honour our connection to Evan and his energetic place in the family. While I don't know the reason why one son lived and another didn't, I have come to accept what is as the providence of God. I am grateful for the chance to know these children and to live life together when it almost never was. And I'm thankful for the loyal and loving family and friends who reminded us that life would go on. Out of hardship, great and good things can happen as the flower finds a way to grow out of the rock. Pain, hopelessness, brokenness, lostness can exist with joy, hope, re-birth, and good at the same time. The wounded place showing us things about the human spirit, healing, change, growth, and finding a different path, a new path. We are getting the fur loved off us like the Velveteen Rabbit and becoming more Real in the process.

That Bittersweetness Is All the Love

This moment in time is hard and painful but good because I am allowing myself to write this part of my story. It's a part that is so tender and treasured, a chapter that has been waiting in a dusty corner until life let me come back to it. I am going to remember the significance of this part of my journey and honour and embrace my pain and my loss. As psychologist Tara Brach puts it, I am going to risk letting myself be seen with "radical acceptance" by embracing the part of me that feels so vulnerable. I will allow the grief to exist for myself and for anyone who it may comfort and encourage. It has been said that nothing is lost in the universe. Everything, including suffering, can transform into something with greater purpose. I feel profoundly humbled that I am part of a vast, loving energy within the intelligent divine plan of the Creator, who comes to us during the times we inhabit our broken places.

As I have been learning to accept my experience, I am embracing the part of myself that worries that the grief is too much after twenty-five years. There is still a part of me that holds an invisible weight of sadness even when the world moves on. This gift of sadness sent me on a search for meaning, in my own life and all of life around me, to understand why things happen that are so painful and unfair. I learned that life is not guaranteed and each day is a new opportunity. Evan's time on earth was brief but meaningful. I hear a small voice in heart say, "Evan, I almost had you for a lifetime where I would get to see you turn into a beautiful person and my heart would burst with love for you. I hold the memory of you in my heart always." When I sit with others who have lost children, we do not say goodbye to them; we make space for them, claiming them as ours. We honour the love that will always exist.

Because the current of life is constantly flowing, I am moved by change, growth, and development toward becoming more of who I am meant to be. It erodes away that which is no longer needed which can be exposing, lonely, and painful at times. Fur was rubbed off and seams were torn, but inside a sawdust heart was changing to stardust and becoming Real. Alive. In my backwards glance, I can see that glimmers of hope were arising in places that had seemed to have had none. More peace was found with knowing that I will see my son again in a Heavenly place. Kindness, laughter, and joy became more beautiful. I might never have known the resilience in me or seen the growth of determination and perseverance without this experience. I developed a patience to wait and to trust.

The Velveteen Rabbit was very wounded in the process of being loved by a small boy. He learned that becoming Real was a "thing that happens to you" over time. Your edges are loved off as you become Real. You are stronger and softer. You are transforming. Just as the wondrous little rabbit was becoming more genuine, more authentically real, we too are in that process. I see that others are missing their button eyes and some of their fur is "loved off," but they have become stronger, deeper, wiser, and more open. Though they are missing their eyes, they are learning to see from within. To be genuine is to be true to your own personality, values, and spirit regardless of the pressure that you are under to be otherwise. We are becoming more of who we are meant to be and evolving the gifts we are meant to bring to the world.

Living with one foot in Heaven and one foot on Earth has sent me on a search to find answers for things that are hard to understand. I wanted to know why sometimes babies don't live, and why there are so many devastating and destructive events that take place. It created a relentless search for meaning inside of me to know why I am here, how I am meant to use what I have experienced to help others, and, more importantly, what the legacy of my loss will be. What can I give to others or give back to life? This ongoing process of living with everyday things while seeing life through more spiritual eyes has been a search for my own unique path of finding truth and meaning in life.

We all come to Earth to have unique and different experiences.

It's okay if my experience doesn't match yours and yours doesn't match mine. They cannot be measured. We are all part of the collective, colourful kaleidoscope that makes up the great tapestry of the human experience. We are living life in all of its splendour and disarray. While we are all walking together, for some it will only be one hour and nineteen minutes and for others it will be longer. But even the smallest number of minutes can change the world.

I have learned that the bittersweetness is all the love. Love always exists despite hate, gain can come out of loss, and joy returns after pain. But love is stronger in the end. Our experience becomes a story of life where we lived and learned to love beyond our trials. Can we let it help others by sharing it in our own unique way to shine a light for even one person?

Your Wound Is the Gateway

It has been said that your wound is the gateway to all that we become as we face adversity of great magnitude. It is the gateway to our unlimited potential to expand and to attract all that is needed to heal and grow. We can stop being ashamed of our wounds, stop judging them, and honour them as they show us who we are and how we are meant to serve. This universal source of Divine spiritual wisdom, the mind of God, that guides us in our "becoming" is always present and holding us.

I see how my journey with grief and loss created compassion and empathy for others who are suffering and need someone to witness and acknowledge their pain. While processing pain with another person can be validating and healing, at the same time I know it can unearth and resurrect other pain from the past and how destabilizing it can be to carry a weight that is not visible. It's a challenge to cope when the world seems to have moved on and every breath feels like a crushing decision to keep living. Other life circumstances had caused some of my grief to be delayed which led to unexpected periods of paralyzing sadness years later. I had no time to process it. There was a part of me that stopped when Evan died. I wish my grief had been neater, tidier, more predictable, but that is not the way of grief—even for a therapist. There is no "right" way to grieve. There is not a defined pathway to recovery. Instead, it's a process with twists and turns taking you forward and backward that will naturally happen over time, just not by the calendar.

Grief comes in many forms and is full of surprises. It pointed out many areas within me that needed work. My grief journey also transformed into something that is greater than me, allowing me to be helpful and empower others as they grieve and go in search of healing. As a therapist, I hear hard things. There is struggle, defeat, sadness, loss, and hopelessness. But it often translates into a lifelong evolution and transformation. Transformation is a complete change in the appearance of something or someone. This is how woundedness prepares us for greater service in the world. This growing ground moves us from comfort to courage to impact. Already made of stardust, we become more light, more encouragement, more acceptance, and more love in the world. I get to bring some measure of acceptance, validation, and hope to another human being, and that reciprocity helps heal me. I feel a deep gratitude for being able to witness something so vulnerable and to see myself in them. It's a chance to provide some of the tender care I needed in my own loss. When others are feeling like they have been abandoned, it helps me see more clearly that would never be the case. My heart tells me that God would be closer to them, as He was to me, in times of faltering faith. I can be a bridge for them to connect with their spirituality and the wisdom and healing that lies within each person. Their stories show me that I am okay, that I am not that different, and that I am human. In those moments, we are the solution for each other. We are healing one another.

I hope I can help my clients go from the "why" to the "what" and "who" they are becoming, and to see their great potential and significance in the world. I draw from the therapy model of Virginia Satir to help people see the internal resources that have provided the strength to withstand life's challenges. Satir's belief is that we all possess the capacity for growth and change within us as well as a connection to spiritual Life energy that helps us survive and even thrive. Stubbornness became determination or perfectionism caused us to turn over every stone to find the solution we needed to survive. When the Rabbit was thrown out onto the trash heap, he had to endure an unexpected and unpredictable journey. In a moment of discouragement, a tear runs down his velvet nose and falls to the ground. A small flower springs up and blossoms in its place, showing life returning. By the end of the book, he was still the same rabbit but more alive, able to leap and run, change, adapt, and embrace a new freedom. He had faced loss, but he was free having been made Real through love.

When life has shaken us, we want to hide to be safe. We don't want others to see we are missing a button eye or a bit of fur. What if we are no longer welcome because of our tattered self? But hiding the wound also hides the place where the light is. Having the courage to unveil ourselves and share bravely who we have become helps encourage others to do the same and to reduce their isolation. That is the sacred gateway: accepting and honouring your story with all its trauma and loss, no matter how big or small. I see how my story went on to deepen and bloom in the subsequent seasons of life. Now I am holding a flashlight for others who are looking for the flowers through their tears.

> *To be a star, you must shine your own light,*
> *follow your own path, and don't worry about*
> *the darkness for that is when stars shine*
> *brightest.*

—Ralph Waldo Emerson

I treasure and cherish that Evan is a part of my experience and my reality. I cry when I miss him and I smile when I see a double rainbow. I am leaning more into my life energy: allowing myself room to grow, finding what I am meant to share and how I am meant to be in the world, embracing the unhealed parts, and finding comfort in healing. I am learning to be okay with feeling broken because life can do that to us sometimes. I have become a soft place for others who feel broken and seek to empower them to find what heals and supports them. I am there to encourage them to listen deeply to their own hearts so they can be nearer to their innate wisdom. To feel deeply, as it is a strength, not a limitation.

There is often a part of us that seeks closure, or a conclusion, to pain and grief after a loss. But my grief has been a companion over many years leading me to this moment in time when I can share my story and reach out to others who are struggling with a loss. Especially, the loss of a child. I have found that the process of grief is actually a pathway to all of the meaningful moments to come. My pain pointed me to a deeper purpose after my loss, a desire to be in service to others and a compassion for others who are struggling to find their way. It inspired me to look for opportunities to collaborate with like-minded people who want to do meaningful things in the world. It created a wish to expand, to grow and to love. While pain will come, it can be healed, integrated, and transformed into powerful inspiration, creativity, and love that can change the world. If grief is the cost of love lost, then let it become the fuel that makes love burn brighter, illuminating the way for others who are seeing the world dimly. Pain through grief is inevitable, but so is the love that grows bigger around it.

    I am grateful for those who have shown themselves to me in their pain because they have helped me heal, they have inspired me, and their strength has encouraged me. They have trusted me to help hold their heart. My prayer is that they know they are not alone as we make our way together with our struggles and in our renewing and healing. If I am here for a reason, as we all are, I hope to make a difference whenever possible, joining my light with others. I find it comforting to believe that the wise and loving universe is conspiring to help us see that we are all beautiful spiritual beings of light in this human experience. I invite you to ask daily, what part of love can I leave, and continue to be a radiant light joining with others through love. In the soulful sentiment of Robert Holden, British psychologist and author, decide to let love be your intention, dedicate yourself to love, and let love inspire you, support you, and guide you.

About Tonda Eger-Chin

Born and raised in Indiana, Tonda Eger-Chin, MS, LPC, RCC studied counselling psychology at Indiana University. She resides in British Columbia, Canada in the Vancouver area with her husband, three children on Earth, and One in Heaven. And two small dogs that make each day better. Tonda has a Master's degree in Counselling Psychology and is a Registered Clinical Counsellor in private practice who works with individuals, couples, and families using a trauma-focused approach with a special interest in grief and loss of a child. She endeavours to grow and expand personally and professionally and continues to offer support and healing for others.

She is proud to have been a board member of the Satir Institute of the Pacific for many years and has been a "student" of Satir Transformational Therapy, as well as a facilitator. She considers herself very fortunate to have studied Neuroscience in the Sand Tray with Madeleine De Little, PhD and continues to do sand tray work with adults and children and perpetuate Madeleine's mission of combining neuroscience with sand tray therapy.

tonda@telus.net
www.instagram.com/@tonda.chin
www.facebook.com/tondachin

www.ingramcontent.com/pod-product-compliance
Lightning Source LLC
Chambersburg PA
CBHW052139070526
44585CB00017B/1897